Inhale

Copyright © 2017 by Colleen Songs

Tellwell Talent

www.tellwell.ca

ISBN

978-1-77370-316-9 (Hardcover)

978-1-77370-315-2 (Paperback)

978-1-77370-317-6 (eBook)

# INHALE

## COLLEEN SONGS

www.colleensongs.ca

# Foreword

In Colleen you meet an elegant woman who embraces you with open arms. Her eyes sparkle with warmth and she has a grace that puts you instantly at ease. This is an iron grace, for you would never know that at one point in her life she was drowning in a whirlpool of pain, torment, and shattered dreams.

Every day with her abusive husband she was pulled deeper and deeper under the surface of the water. Instead of letting the currents claim her, Colleen finally pushed her way up to the air. She didn't use force to free herself. She didn't use unkindness. She found strength by remembering the strong foundation her parents had once built for her and her siblings. She remembered her children and how much she loved them. She remembered that even though she had married a man she loved, he was no longer a husband.

Colleen's words are honest.

She does not play the "blame game." She tells you all the unflattering bits about herself too.

This isn't a one-sided story. It's a story about how complicated we human beings are but also how we all simply want to be loved.

Colleen's mission is to share her story in the hopes it could help someone, maybe even you.

She takes us through her journey from a young mother who falls in love, to a woman whose life starts to crumble, to a wife crushed by her husband, and finally to a woman who uses her iron grace to transcend tragedy.

This is Colleen's story.

But it could also be Your mother's.

Or Your Daughter's.

Or Yours.

Lea Storry, Our Corporate History

403-700-5435

www.ourcorporatehistory.ca • www.ourfamilylines.ca

*Your bricks and mortar in words*

# With Gratitude

A journey through such adversity comes with an entourage of 'roadies'.

Throughout this story I use pseudonyms for my 'roadies' to allow them free access to come and go without judgment or labels from the outside world.

I would not be here today without them.

I am so grateful for:

My Children. For some crazy reason You chose me to be your Momma and take this journey along with me.

Thank You for guiding me and for your Souls' knowing when it was time to 'take a detour' in order to be safe and await my return from my life's 'detour'; for the other direction we may not have recovered.

My Siblings, especially 'Ester'. Your blunt, love-filled honesty keeps me brave.

My niece and best friend, 'Mae'. You are my soul sanctuary and a believer in me always, all ways.

My writing mentor, Steven Ross Smith.

Your generous read-through and tips helped to make my story speak to its reader. "Epic!" you said.

My fellow Migratory 'Wordsmiths' of Canmore, Alberta. You give me a safe place to reap feedback, chapter by chapter.

My friend, Lea Storry of Family Lines. You helped me to structure this story from its birthing. Thank you for your kind balance and insight.

And to quote my additional Readers:

Farhana Dhalla, friend/author of 'Thank You For Leaving Me': *"Your pen should never leave the paper."*

Janis Doherty, marketing expert/friend: *"I'm so inspired by you and your power!"*

Sandy Larson, marketing expert/friend: *"Wow – I sat down this afternoon with the intention to read a chapter or two of the book. Four hours later – unable to stop reading…"*

Lynne Rach, newspaper reporter/TV producer: *"Upon first meeting I saw the hooded eyes of a broken woman; today that woman smiles. Her story offers hope to those in despair; offers the certainty that "this too shall pass."*

For Klement Danda and WomenTalk, Calgary: You helped me talk about this for the first time through word and song.

For my Tellwell Team. Thank you for taking me 'Canadiana' all the way. For listening to and guiding me with this piece of art, and for your light-hearted patience with my savvy 'Word' skills.

For 'Jayne' and 'Sweetpea', my Guardian Angels: You took me in, fattened me up, and gave me sanctuary.

And for my 'Present': You found me and provide me a safe place to finally call home and write.

With love, Colleen

I dedicate this book to my Children.

You heard my prayers from a distance
and drew me home to You safely
through your
graceful,
wise love
and
forgiveness.

I love You.
xoxo Momma

# The Journey

# CHAPTER 1

## Running through the Cornfields

"I didn't know then what love really was but I
am definitely finding out what it isn't.
I am awakening from the fog."
– Colleen Songs

It is so hot.
I pause and wipe the sweat off my brow, taking a slow deep breath
to get through another day.
Hot and suffocating.
The sticky-sweet, cicada humming of the Virginia summer heat
clings to my skin.
But that's not what's suffocating me.
Revulsion is choking me,
strangling my dreams
and turning them into nightmares.

I had loved the South even before I had ever seen it.
Since I first read *Gone with the Wind* as a child in Canada and
wrapped my imagination in its romantic history and fiction it
had been a goal to come here one day, to experience life in the
Southern States.
Just not like this.
Every promise he made convincing me to take this trip with him
breaks with every mile of the odometer.
He is no different than he was at home.
I'm only farther and farther away from it.

My thoughts wander as I stand at the sink.
Washing dishes after another silent breakfast, I watch my hands
perform their monotonous duties.
*This life no longer seems real.*
I place another plate in its assigned space.
*It did at one time,*
*a very long time ago,*
*when it was just me and the Children.*
*Why didn't I see how perfectly quiet and serene that time was?*
*Time I can never get back now!*

I ached for like-minded companionship, something I didn't have
with my Children's father; the kind of love that celebrated my
talents, lifted my spirits, encouraged my dreams.
But I wasn't patient enough to wait for it, or wise enough to know
the value of a 'good for me' kind of love in order to have a 'good
for me' kind of life.
So I settled for easy love.
This kind.
Where I do all the loving, and fixing, and nurturing, and, and, and?
*Yep.*
*This love.*
I glance over at my husband.
Sitting in his chair.
Watching the news.
*What a fool I was!*
*I didn't know then what love really was but I am definitely finding out what
it isn't.*
*This love isn't the good for me kind.*


It is July 2009.
I have just turned forty-one.
We have been married for almost five years and I have known him
for eight.
At first he adored the Children.
He had none of his own and yearned to be part of a family.
I couldn't see that he was incapable of the task until my little family
was torn to pieces by the dynamics he had been raised in.
Alcohol.
Abuse.
Narcissism.
On top of all that, he has been recently diagnosed with Bipolar 1
Disorder: an answer to his years of debilitating mental struggles,

attempted suicides, and trauma that he foisted upon my Children
and me; a precursor to our yet undetermined fate.

With the Children safely at their dad's, this trip South is meant to
bring us back together,

to get him well,

to rebuild a life in ruins.

But it's tearing us further apart

moment by moment.

The Fifth Wheel we're travelling in has become a cell and I am as
much his prisoner as he is a prisoner to his personality and disease.

I put the last of the dishes away in the cupboard.

The oppressive heat only adds to the pressure inside the RV.

Nestled within the gated Virginia campground, one would never
guess the anguish behind the doors of the Alberta-plated truck and
Fifth Wheel.

*I have to get out of here.*

The confined space reeks with the vile scent of stale vodka stirring
with his negative emotional poison.

*I have to get out of here!*

"I need to go for a run, James," I say, trying to sound cheerful. I
do not want him to suspect anything nor offer to join me. "I can't
believe I'm really here." I hang the dishtowel on the hook beneath
the sink. "I want to take it all in. I'll be back in a bit. Just enjoy
some you-time, okay?"

*Smile.*

*Look him in the eye and smile.*

"Pretty hot, isn't it?" he asks, staring at me blankly.

Sitting there,

in his chair,

rocking.

He hasn't even showered yet.

It's way past ten o' clock and he used to shower upon waking.

His once brilliant, blue eyes are now sallow and grey.
His once sturdy and fit body is hidden by a drinker's belly and baggy t-shirt to try and hide the evidence.
*Where did you go?*
So empty of life.
So ready to charge at me if I give him the slightest sign of leaving, or any cause of suspicion that I may be trying to get away.
"You know me," I say brightly. "I love the heat and I need to move after that long drive. Don't worry; I'll be okay."
I quickly pack my running pouch with tissue and ChapStick to make it obvious that I'm leaving everything else behind.
No water.
No change.
If I take these things he will think I will find a phone to make a call or buy water at the gate, which means a longer run and the possibility of my leaving him.
A lesson learned from what he interpreted as an attempt to leave him that caused him to throw his drinking glass at my feet.

I took a little too long on a run during one of our overnight rest stops.
Lost and grieving my Children, beginning to awaken to the darkness of the situation I was in, I simply took an unusually long time trying to figure out my emotions and fears.
He walked around the rest area campsite in a panic that I had left him and eventually found me quite a distance from our campsite.
He took me by the arm and led me back into the RV, shutting the door behind us.
As I slipped off my runners (he hated me tracking dirt into the living space, though he kept his own shoes on), I tried to explain.
I had just lost track of time!
I was missing home already!
I needed to call my Children!

He raged on and on about not being able to trust me any longer,
calling me a two-faced 'c'-word,
telling me I was selfish for not understanding how much he loved me,
that he needed my support right now.
He blamed my Children for causing all of our stress.
As he shifted his weight from side to side while expressing his
fury, he reached for a glass and threw it on the floor between us to
emphasize his disappointment in me.
I purposely went on several short walks or runs throughout the
following days to prove I'd always return without any further cause
to worry.
I would soak my feet after each excursion.
I had fine slivers of glass in my toes for days.
In front of him I'd roll my eyes at myself when he'd bring up my
'moment of weakness' to 'cave-in' to the 'old habits' of "always
putting my kids' needs before our own".
Hoping he would relax and forget about it.
Hoping I would eventually have another window of opportunity to
linger away from him, or better yet, to keep running.

I'm out the door before he says anything else.
*I'm forgetting something.*
I hesitate before stepping into my run.
*Just run.*
*He is no longer worried about you leaving.*

I linger another moment,
drained from this unnatural state of being on edge all the time,
frustrated that my mind is always so foggy.
*What is it that I'm forgetting?*
Anxious that he'll follow me out the door, I shrug away the knot in
my stomach.
I put one foot in front of the other.

I find my pace,
slow and easy at first.
*Just run.*
I give in to my thoughts.
The relief of getting away from him frees my mind, at least for
a while.
I pick up my pace,
welcoming the impact of my feet on the ground.
The pain in my legs from sitting too long in the truck on our long
drive from Alberta soon disappears.
I beg Virginia to forgive me for bringing his sordid energy to
its beauty.
I breathe in the humid, sultry air.
Out here it's a welcoming embrace.
My ears take in the humming forest and my eyes brighten at the
lush green landscapes.
I run.
I pass a pond thick with lily pads and bobbing turtle heads.
I giggle with delight.
*How adorable you are!*
I run.
"Hello!" I whisper to the heavy, ivy-cloaked trees lining the
pathway like big, verdant giants. "Thank you for your presence on
this run."
The trees make me feel safe.
Guarded.
Matching my breath to the rhythm of each step, I keep on.
Up the slopes,
over slugs,
and into the fields of cotton and corn.
*Cotton.*
*So that's what a cotton field looks like up close!*
I stop to catch my breath.

I look at the knee-high shrubs to see how they could be harvested.
Tiny bundles of white are set like diamonds in prongs of thorns.
*How fitting.*
*I know exactly how you feel.*
I don't touch them as they aren't mine to touch.
I don't want to infect them with any negative, energetic charge I
may be carrying.
I scan the fields and see an old yellow farmhouse with red and
white outbuildings in the distance.
I imagine a time, before machinery, when the cotton pickers' hands
would have been cut and splintered from this harvest.
*What a terrible job picking cotton would have been!*
I feel pain from splinters too, but of a different kind.
*Will I ever be able to stop walking on eggshells?*
*Will I ever be able to leave this man?*
*Will I ever love again?*
*Will I ever be loved by someone as much as I love them?*
*Will I end up cutting any hand that promises to love me when this is over?*
I breathe in the diffused scent of cotton.
It isn't the scent of sun drenched linen, but rather of a fluffy puff
of dirt.
Raw.
Delicate.
Natural.
I breathe out fear.
I breathe in my present moment of freedom.
I run.
I am met next by a corn field planted so closely along the edge of
the path that I can feel the soil-scented breeze rippling heavily
through the stalks.
Tears start running down my face as an urge to escape comes to
me once again.
*If I were to run through the field and get lost, would he find me?*

*Would I be able to make it home to Alberta on my own?*
I run through a few rows along the side of the road.
*This feels delicious.*
I'm hidden.
Protected.
My heart beats with excitement.
*Yes!*
My pace quickens.
*Run through the field!*
*He'll never find you here!*
*Run to the farmhouse and ask to use the phone.*
*Call Wayne and ask to talk to the Children!*
Wayne.
My Children's father.
The one person I could rely on to offer a safe place for our
Children when my home became too dangerous.
*Wayne will understand once I tell him the truth;*
*once I tell him I HAD to leave to protect them all;*
*once I tell him I had to send Sissy back to him for her own safety;*
*once I tell the Children what I was protecting them from.*
*Oh, to talk to my Children!*
I weave through the stalks and rows.
*Once I tell them Mommy's sorry;*
*once I tell them I'm coming home;*
*once I tell them it's no use,*
*he'll never be better!*
*Wayne will send money to get me home!*
*Wayne will save me!*
*He will understand and get me out of here.*
I keep running, but my earlier hesitation reveals itself.
*My passport!*
**"NO!"** I cry out.
I stumble to a stop.

**"NO!"** I berate myself.

Days before I hid my passport.

I put it in one of the outer pockets of the RV for this moment when I had the chance to run.

*Why didn't I take my passport?*

*Why didn't I listen to my gut when it told me I had forgotten something?*

*I'm no good at being sneaky!*

*If I had my passport, I could leave right now!*

"What's the use?" I reason bitterly to the cornstalks as though they are the jury I call 'myself'.

*Do you really think Wayne will help you?*

*He probably hates you!*

*And James will track you down anyway.*

*Worse, he'll call Wayne and start his cutting, verbal abuse and you'll be dead before you can get home to the Children!*

After three actual attempts on his own life since we had met, and his new temper tantrums which involve throwing things at me, I am uncertain as to when he will combine the two.

He threatens my life with words like "I couldn't live without you!" and "I couldn't bear to think of you with another man!"

**"STUPID!"** I scream to the corn, beating my fists into my knees.

My tears fall and the cornstalks quiver.

They're afraid for me too.

I don't know how long I stand in the field,

weeping and cursing,

trying to avoid hopelessness.

I only awaken when everything feels calm again.

I breathe in the scent of the corn.

I feel the soil beneath my feet.

I pray for the earth to send my Children a message

in a dream,

in a thought,

ANYTHING to tell them I love them,

and that I'm coming home.
*Somehow, I am coming home!*
I run a little more before turning around.
I find my breath and time it once again to the rhythm of my feet.
I calm myself with thoughts of home as I head back to the
Fifth Wheel.
*Leave no trace of tears.*
*You can get through today, one more day.*
I run.
*Work on the plan.*
*One more day is all.*
I wipe the tears with the hem of my t-shirt.
*The Children will know you're coming home.*
*The Children know you love them.*
I run.

# CHAPTER 2

## Where did he Go?

"…there he was.
The man who would be the mason of this fortress I now call me."
— Colleen Songs

I'm back at the RV.

As soon as I see him my thoughts of freedom melt to mush in the stifling heat.

He's standing outside, smoking a cigarette.

Arms crossed over his chest,

jaw set,

eyes glaring.

I feel his body language more than I read it, and as I walk closer to him his darkness envelops me.

"That was a little long, wasn't it?" he asks me.

He takes a drag, slowly spewing smoke and negativity in the air between us.

I wipe the sweat off my face and smile through the filthy cloud.

"It's so nice here I lost track of time," I cheer. "I saw a cotton field up the road. I've never seen one before."

*Keep pretending everything is fine.*

*Distract his distracted mind.*

I scoot into the trailer before he replies.

I gather my shower bag and bathing suit before heading to the pool.

I shower there now whenever I can.

I don't want him seeing my body anymore.

He hasn't seen it in years anyway.

He's in the RV now, standing at the bottom of the three steps that lead up to the bedroom.

Waiting.

I turn to leave the travelling house again.

"I'm going to the pool to soak before I get sore," I tell him, "and then we can eat and go wherever you wish, okay?"

He stands there blocking me.

To try and grab my passport now would be futile.

I was gone too long and now he's in hover mode.

I lost my moment of escape.

"Why do you stay, Colleen?" he growls suspiciously. "Why don't
you go back to your ungrateful kids and make more excuses
for them?"
He's in need of fighting his demons, pushing me to challenge him
into action.
I know these words all too well.
Yelling will soon follow,
spitting,
guttural,
vicious yelling,
accompanied by flying objects
and lethal threats.
His cheeks are flushed and I can feel the heat from his body radiate
like a pustule sore.
My Daughter and my Son!
All I can do is stand there as my tears begin to well.
His words impale my heart one more time.


My Son was the first to go.
We moved him to his dad's when he turned twelve.
I saw it coming.
The locking of horns between James, the step-father; and Andrew,
a boy coming of age in a household that was starting to unravel.
It was a recipe for disaster.
*My Son.*
*My gentle giant.*
I knew his tender heart would not survive the battle when it began,
not with this man.
We made the decision as a family – my Son, his dad, and I – to
move Andrew back to his dad's at a time when a boy needs his
father, a good man.
Not this one.

Not this man who called my boy a wimp when he choked on a chip
and cried from the pain of swallowing.

Pain that wouldn't stop and caused me to rush him to the hospital,
where I found out he had a hole in the back of his throat caused by
that chip and only hours to live if I hadn't gotten him there when
I did.

No.

This was not the man I wanted to lead my Son into manhood.

*I should have sent you packing, not moved my Son!*

*My Daughter.*

*Sissy.*

She was only sixteen and discovering herself in a new town and a
new school.

She fit right in.

She was welcomed as though she had always been there.

She wowed her art teacher with her talent.

She won over our neighbours with her devotion to horses.

Her sixteenth birthday gift was a four-year-old sorrel gelding, Jet.

She tended to her horse every day as promised.

It was a year of firsts for her:

her first horse

her first year of dating,

her first boyfriend.

But James disapproved of the boy who caught her eye.

There were fights and public embarrassment caused by her stepfa-
ther's imaginary fears and loss of control.

He remedied the situation by sending her to her dad's for spring
break, and then never letting her back into my life.

Making that phone call was torture for me,

with James breathing down my neck,

to 'tell her, or he would'

that she wasn't welcome home;

losing consciousness and reality,

crawling on the floor as I packed her room,
trying to salvage what remained of her precious belongings
before he could destroy them all with his temper;
knowing my Children would hate me.
*What mother leaves her children?*
We just stand there,
eye to eye
as memories float rapidly through my mind
and tears fall from my eyes.
*One who feels she has no choice.*
*Their safety is her everything.*
Driving away from their dad's house after dropping off my
Daughter's things, I clawed at the window of the car.
My Children faded into the distance.
I was desperate to hold them, protect them, to tell them I loved
them.
He would hurt them all if I told them the truth.
So I couldn't.
I feared for their lives and for mine and I didn't have the words to
explain my dread.
I was shot down when I did ask for help
from family,
from friends,
from Wayne,
from doctors and therapists.
I was accused of being weak, and made to feel ashamed to break
another marriage.
I only knew that I had to protect my Children.
I had to deal with this monster first in order for all of us to be
safe again,
to be a family again,
without a beast threatening to tear us apart.

"See what they've done to you!" he rages in answer to my tears.

He always blames my Children for his demented mentality.

Now here in Virginia, his words once again plunge knives into my chest.

Always cutting us.

Never digging into himself.

Blaming my Children, never himself.

We remain at a standstill for what feels like hours with me at the top of the bedroom stairs, he at the base.

I need to stay calm.

*Tread carefully.*

*There are no more words.*

*Words only fuel the voices in his head.*

"I'm going to the pool." I break the stalemate, pushing myself forward down the stairs.

I slip on my sandals and reach for the door.

I steel myself for the threats and accusations that I know will follow any challenge.

"You'll never see them again," he says.

His voice bites into the back of my neck.

"I never want them in my home again," he continues. "I hate your kids. They don't care about me. Remember what they did to you? What they're doing to us? They're spoiled, and Wayne just backs them. He's useless. They'll amount to nothing, you know!"

He steps closer to me, so close I smell the cigarettes on his breath.

It's putrid and I fight the tears about to spill.

Tears do me no favours.

"The Children have done nothing to us, you PRICK! YOU have torn us apart!" I turn to burst at him.

*He is so far gone.*

*So past help.*

*So past hope.*

*So many have tried to help him.*

He once was a vibrant spirit who loved life, loved people,
helped others.
He taught me about spirituality and unlabelled faith.
He once laughed with my Children.
He once wrapped us all up in adventure and surprises.
That man is gone.
Gone.
My sister once told me, during one of her warning conversations,
that we are our true selves in sickness or when we're drunk.
I shrugged her off then.
But now, now I see it.
*He is his true self:*
*a self-centred,*
*narcissistic*
*addict.*
You can't fight nor argue with that.
That part of him will only kill me before I can reunite with
my Children.
I look at him with pity,
vying hatred against compassion.
He is so gone.
*Was I that blind before?*
*Was this all a ruse?*

I had met him nine years earlier, a high energy businessman who
took my breath away one afternoon as I sat in the waiting room of
the doctor's office.
I knew he was trouble by the twinge in my gut, but the flutter in
my heart told me he would be in my life somehow.
I was newly single, though long separated from Wayne, my
first husband.
Wayne is a good man.
We had just married too young.

Family expectations and guilt-ridden obligations took us from
where we should have remained to where we felt we had to be.
I'll never regret our marriage and he still remains my friend.
Without him I would never have had my two Children.
Between the first time and the last time James Edwards' blue eyes
held mine, my life would change forever.
It was not usually this busy at the doctor's office.
The waiting room was too large for the small-town population of
Pearson, Alberta.
I had both of my Children on my lap, barely eight and six at
the time.
They chatted and cuddled close to me as we waited for the doctor.
They always snuggled into me.
I loved them.
I adored them.
I protected them.
I looked around the room, wondering how it could be so busy
and if there were really that many people in this small little
town when...
there he was.
The man who would be the mason of this fortress I now call 'me'.
The only other seat available was the one right beside mine.
Looking back on our first meeting, I naively saw this as a 'sign'.
"Is this seat taken?" Blue Eyes asked me.
"No, go ahead. It's busy in here today." Flustered, I held my
Children closer.
"Momma," my Daughter whispered, her little hand turning my
cheek to look into her huge brown eyes, "you shouldn't talk to
strangers, Momma."

# CHAPTER 3

## A Song of Tears

"My fingers find a melody
and they mourn."
– Colleen Songs

I return to the bedroom and close the sliding door between us to
escape his glare and cutting words.
I hear him in his rocker,
rocking fervently.
The creaking of his chair is as agitated as his mood.
I feel my body backing into the corner of the room.
I sink to the floor by my closet door.
This is my safe zone.
Hidden inside the drawers and beneath my clothes are pictures of
my Children in a little silver folding frame.
I press my back against the drawers.
I dare not take the photos out and touch them for fear he'll catch
me and then destroy them.
I simply feel their presence instead.
He cannot take my thoughts from me.
He cannot take my vision from me.
He cannot take my Children from my mind.
I feel their ties and they give me courage.
I reach for my guitar case.
My pretty guitar fits perfectly beneath the overhanging mattress in
the Fifth Wheel loft.
She's my best friend.
She'll help me find my way out of here.
She'll help me sing my way out of this nightmare.
I wrap her strap around me and start to strum.
My fingers know her by memory.
Her tone sends waves of love throughout my body.
I feel my Children's arms grasping each note to embrace me.
I succumb to the tears.
Cradled in love and rhythm I feel a song,
a song welling up from the marrow of my secret self.
*He is already gone.*
*There is no use.*

*There is no love left in him to give.*
*He is lost to us.*
*Babies, Momma tried.*
*We all tried!*
My fingers find the melody and they mourn…
for the life we could have had,
for the life I thought we would have.
I hear him mumbling as he scrambles outside for another cigarette.
*My husband is gone.*
*He is more like a patient, and I his caregiver.*
*The only way home is to take care of him, one day at a time.*
*One day at a time.*
The Alcoholics Anonymous mantra he once preached with passion
comes to my mind.
The reality of what I'll be facing with this man in the weeks, possibly months ahead rises up to stare me down.
*It's going to be a long climb, but I know who is at the summit.*
*I'm coming home to you, my Babies.*
I think of all the men and women of the American Civil War
grounds where we've been touring on his good days.
*This is my own civil war; I am torn between vows and bondage.*
This is my own Gettysburg:
the rebel yell,
the marching troops,
the horses burdened,
the fear of what lies ahead,
leaders planning strategies,
tasked with protecting the lives of their soldiers,
yet sending them to their demise in the name of duty.
I hear the drums.
I hear the wagons and rattling of metal.
I hear the gunfire.
I know what's ahead of me, and it drives me forward.

I know it's not going to be as easy as I had hoped.
I know I am as much to blame as he is.
*I let him into our life.*
*This is my cross to bear.*
I strum my guitar as tears drop like notes on paper.
*I cannot have his blood on my hands.*
*I know he'll kill himself and then leave me with the mess.*
*How could I live with myself?*
*How could I live with that nightmare when life is so valuable to me?*
*How would I get back home?*
*My family name would be dishonoured by media, news, and shame.*
*Is this the mountain I had to climb to discover my worth?*
*It's up to me to give this experience purpose.*
*I'm going to take this hill.*
And then the words of a song come to me:

> Looks like there's a mountain
> rising right in front of us.

*I never imagined this love would be so hard.*
*That this bright-eyed, spiritually awake person would be lost to such darkness.*

> It's hard to see the sky above,
> or the trees for lack of trust.

*My Children and I offered ourselves to this man;*
*this man who promised so many things and tried so hard at times that we*
*actually believed him.*

> You're telling me you're not so sure
> we're gonna make it up this time.

*There is nothing we, the Children and I, didn't do to make the best of things, to*
*try our very best to make it work.*
*I am responsible for letting him go and letting us live.*

All I can do is take you where
you're on your own to climb.

*I can do this.*
*For every tear my Children and I have shed, I WILL do this.*
*With as much heart as I gave to him in the first place, I WILL do this!*

Baby, I can take this hill!
I can take another day!
Even if it's higher than
it was yesterday.

*I will never allow us to be hurt again.*
*I WILL carry this burden and I WILL carry it to the summit.*

I followed you through every fear
but now you've crossed the line

*I release the fear.*
*I release my marriage vows as I make new ones to myself.*
*I allow courage.*
*I allow strength.*
*I allow love.*
*Oh the power of Love!*

Baby, I can take this hill,
take it one day at a time.

There is still doubt and angst over what lays ahead, but — as usual —
the gift of my talent guides me to a peaceful state of being.
Tears run down my face, my neck.
I sing the song over and over through whispery sobs.
Shifting the lyrics to fit the rhythm of my despair I recreate
my strategy.
*I'm now only a guardian and he is my patient.*
I reset my mind.
*Only God can help him now.*
*I will bring him, my patient, to where he needs to be so God can take over.*
*Then I can slip away burden-free, debt-free, as I ascend through whatever I am*
*meant to learn by living this journey.*
*I know what my patient will do if I make any more attempts to leave.*
*I resign myself to finding him a safe place, where he'll be content long enough for*
*me to leave him unattended, without suspicion.*
*It'll be a safe place where I won't have his blood on my conscience nor my own*
*blood shed by his fear.*
*Forgive him, for he knows not what he does.*
I nestle my pretty guitar down inside her case and thank the giver
of that sacred space called talent.
I step into the ensuite of my bedroom and splash my face
with water.
I don my bathing suit and cover.
I grab my towel and open the bedroom door.
I step down into the living room.
He is no longer rocking in his incessant chair.
He is outside smoking.
I make a snack to take with me and leave a plate of food for him.

## CHAPTER 4

# A Little Glimpse of Why

"I wonder how we appear
to the strangers around us."
– Colleen Songs

He comes to the pool and quietly makes himself at ease on
the lounge chair beside me, fussing to make sure everything
is just right.
He makes sure there's no wrinkle in his towel and then carefully
gets out his stuff.
Each item is set in ascending height order on the table beside him.
Glasses.
  Book.
    Sunscreen.
      Water bottle.
He ebbs into quiet as he finds his comfy spot.
I notice once again how he has let himself go.
His bipolar medications give his once rippling core a swollen belly.
This, combined with a seasoning of the skin from the abuse of tan
beds, smoking, and alcohol, gives him a haggard, leathery look.
He is usually hyperactive, edgy, and anal about everything
around him.
He needs control of his environment to silence his worries and
stresses and those imaginary ever-speaking voices in his head that
exhaust both him and those around him.
But for now, I notice my patient is calm.
I assess him briefly:
no twitching feet,
no set jaw,
no restlessness as he breathes in the sun
and the heat
and the scent of the day.
I sigh with gratitude for the emotional reprieve and I let the
anxiety leave my body.
I don't know how long we simply sit in silence together, apart.
I simply let it happen.
I wonder how we appear to strangers.
I place my book down and slip into the shallow end of the pool.

He remains lounging in silence.

There's only one other couple and they're at the deep end talking while their children laugh and dive after pool toys.

It's a beautiful oasis.

The grounds are spacious, lush, and quiet.

I rest my chin atop my arms on the side of the pool and welcome the water lapping upon my skin.

The morning run, the impact of his words, and his threats slowly dissipate into the air.

I ask the coolness of the water to wash away this morning's pain of body and spirit.

I ask it to help me take on my new mission to get through each day.

One day at a time.

*This too shall pass.*

I'm wearing a new bathing suit.

I rarely have anything new for myself nowadays.

I bought it for myself on our one daytrip to Virginia Beach.

It was my birthday.

He didn't remember it.

Multi shades of abstract amethyst and pink caught my eye in the store window.

The white trim and strings are tied bright against my honey-bronzed, southern sun-kissed skin.

A little girl comes to our side of the pool.

"You have a pretty bathing suit," she says to me. "Mine's pink. Want to watch me play?"

She jumps into the water before I can answer.

A true compliment.

I am humbled and grateful.

"That was amazing!" I praise her hopeful face as she surfaces.

She takes me back to times of watching my own Children playing in the pool.

"Watch us, Momma! Watch us!" they would chime in unison.

I look over to my patient as a lump forms in my throat.

He's turned around on the lounger to lie on his stomach, facing the pool.

He's watching the little girl with delight.

His eyes are awake,

clear,

and present.

*There he is.*

*James.*

"You are so beautiful," he offers softly as his gaze returns to me.

He has told me a few times over the course of dating that he found me an 'odd sort of plain'; that my personality and loving heart made me pretty.

I see myself as the best I can be and make efforts to keep myself healthy and fit, but I don't see myself as beautiful.

So those rarely spoken words shock me.

I smile and shrug my shoulders, not sure how else to respond.

"Why do you stay?" he asks quietly, sincerely. "You do know I miss the way things were, and I miss the kids when we were all happy."

His words attempt to reassure me that he knew we were once happy as he points in the direction of the little girl.

"I'm just so messed-up, Colleen. I don't want to be like this. I see you and you're beautiful. When I first saw you sitting there holding the kids at the doctor's office I thought, 'Wow! Would I love to have THAT in my life.' "

He wipes his eyes.

From somewhere inside I feel a twinge of hope for him on this quest to be well again,

longing for what should have been,

grieving for what could have been.

Perhaps due to my new focus I feel safe enough to try and remember why I have stayed with him.

*Why have I stayed?*

I smile.

"Sissy said I shouldn't talk to strangers," I say. "It took her months to even smile at you."

By the softness in his eyes I feel that he is fondly reminiscing, so I continue, "But she did in time. Remember that storm we watched on the deck at my place? You came over for dinner. She peeked around the corner spying on us and then jumped between us on the couch and just sat there all bossy and chatty."

We both laugh.

*Could this be the start of a healthy, loving, accepting goodbye?*
*Our vows were, after all, "As long as we both shall live in love."*
*When we wrote our vows, I was very aware of the words.*
*Now I know why.*
*Intervention.*

In answer to his question of why I stay, I decide to share the memory that keeps me, kept me, trying and hoping.

I was raised to take marriage seriously;

to know that there would be good and bad times;

to know that people change and grow;

to know that it was work to be married.

Mostly I was shown that it was the thought behind the deed and the motive behind the action that either kept you in a marriage or rushed you out.

"Remember that first trip you took to Cortes Island? With Rob?" I ask him.

Rob.

Dear Rob.

A tall, sweet friend with whom James went to AA.

They had planned a Buddhist workshop/retreat together at a spiritual learning centre in British Columbia.

I had never heard of it at the time and James had promised to take me there one day.

"We were just dating and you had the trip planned already. You were so excited to go. You were only gone for a week, but on the day of your return you left early and drove sixteen hours straight to come back and surprise us. Rob wondered what the heck you were doing. Remember?"

Tightness grows in my throat but I keep my voice light.

Talking about the memory brings me right back to that moment.

I remember the flush of surprise as his kiss woke me in the middle of the night.

I remember feeling touched that he drove non-stop just to get home to me.

He smiles as I search his face.

"You said you couldn't wait to get back to us, the Children and me, and that you had never felt this way before. You even brought gifts home for the Children. They were delighted."

Silence.

Silence for a few moments.

"That's why I stayed," I choke back a few tumbling tears. "You said *us*."

The ripples of the pool shimmer and dance around me.

"Yeah," he whispers.

I kick back to float in the water, cooling my head.

Then I slip back to the shade of the pool side.

I feel a tiny sense of hope for a breakthrough from this madness.

*I hope this peaceful moment never ends.*

Then, before my eyes, he disappears.

His face tenses,

his lips tighten,

he stares at me,

bores holes through me.

The pool water turns icy cold.

I start to shiver.

Goosebumps prickle my skin.

*He's gone.*
*Oh my God!*
*What's in his mind now?*
*There will be no beautiful goodbye!*
He gets up from the lounge chair in a rush and gathers his things.
He's my patient again.
I step out of the pool and wrap myself tightly in my towel.
"What's wrong?" I ask. "Are you okay? Did you forget your meds?"
I scramble to pick up my things and follow him out.
I am not sure where his mind is.
I am not sure what he is about to say or do in front of
these children.
"Your useless, ungrateful kids," he spits, "couldn't care less
about me! Everything I did for them! They've ruined us and all
you do is miss them and defend them. I know you want to call
them, Colleen!"
He's shouting now and I am frozen.
"Go ahead and call them," he shouts. "CALL THEM! But you'll
never SEE them again. I won't have them in my life ever!"
He stomps away, cursing me under his breath.
The family is watching.
They gather their children away from us.
We've tainted their beautiful day.
The pool is silent.
I am embarrassed and surrender to the darkness that has now
swum over us.
We pack up the RV and head north.
Back home to Canada.

# CHAPTER 5

## Feet on the Dashboard

"Honey, it's going to hurt if you do
or hurt if you don't.
But if you do,
you'll get stronger and be
ahead of the game."
– Colleen Songs

A country station plays on the radio.

The only words between us are sung by strangers through the silence.

His jaw is set and the window is down to let his cigarette smoke escape.

*Go ahead and smoke.*

*Smoke your lungs into a black tarry sack of exhalation!*

Over miles and miles of highway, the beautiful New York state landscape passes in a blur.

I escape into its mystery.

*Who are the people enjoying these beautiful historic little towns?*

*My Son would love to know the history.*

*Oh! There is a horse.*

*A horse!*

My Daughter loves horses.

The sight of the grazing horse in the field on the side of the road tugs me back into a pool of regret.

My heart squeezes in my chest.

My hand finds my chest to soothe the aching sob that is my heart's beat.

*How can I make the wheels go backwards?*

*How can I go back in time?*

*Instead of giving in to his pleas to take this trip, I would pack his bags and lock my doors and still have my home and Children and life!*

I close my eyes.

My neck hurts from constantly facing my window but I can't stand to look at him.

I stretch my legs and rest my feet up on the dashboard because he hates it when I do that.

He stares at me with disapproval.

*I don't care.*

*I am like a bird in a cage trying to get out!*

*I will never get a pet bird.*

My legs are swelling from the heat and the extra long hours of
sitting in this truck as we drive away his tantrum.
I make a point of stretching my legs out and rubbing them vigor-
ously to feel the blood flowing again.
*One word and I will jump out of this truck!*
*I will tuck and roll into anything else but him.*
I giggle at the idea of my bravery.
*God will not let me die.*
*I think He enjoys torture more.*
*He has let me live this far, so bring it on, driver.*
I laugh at myself.
*I am going nutso!*
Holding my stomach, I laugh out loud.
The laughter wells up deep inside me like I've struck oil.
"What's so funny?" he asks, aggravated that I could possibly be
happy about something.
*How dare I be laughing when he is upset?*
I laugh harder.
Then I remember my Mother.
She laughed herself happy in times of trouble.


I remember the day the bank came and took my Dad's car away
after he had to sign over the saw mill that he had put his everything into.
All their dreams and money, gone, with three children still at home
to feed and clothe and put through school.
How did she find it within herself to laugh?
Laughter was her personal therapy.
Dad looked out the living room window,
watching the car disappear,
tears in his eyes,
failure in his heart.
I held onto his hand and told him of my love and belief in him.

Mom sat on the sofa and got the giggles,
giggles that turned to laughter,
laughter that turned to tears,
tears that turned to more laughter,
laughter that brought Dad, my Sisters and I to her side
ending up in a pile of hugs
and tears
and laughter on the floor.
*That woman could laugh the ego out of the Devil!*
And Dad,
in all his shattered pride,
smiled through his tears and told us that
"All that really matters fits right here in these old arms of mine."

The more I laugh, the more my patient grows agitated.
He speeds up.
He thinks that daring our lives with speed will frighten me
into submission.
This has been his tactic from the moment we pulled away
from home.
The more I laugh, the angrier he gets, and the faster he drives.
*Awe, he's ticked right off.*
I can't stop laughing.
*Here we go again.*
*Whatever!*
Pulling a twenty-nine-foot Fifth Wheel on the narrow, shoulder-
less highways of the upper Eastern States is precarious enough,
never mind at the speed he is climbing to now.
I glance over at the speedometer.
One hundred thirty kilometres per hour!
*Getting close to the edge there, buddy!*

"Go ahead and speed till we crash," I find my voice challenging him. "Come on! Let's see what this diesel can do. Come on! Let's die in the U.S. of A.! We'll make the news!"

I can't stop laughing.

*God, I am going insane!*

*His insanity is rubbing off on me!*

"Let's end it here and now," I say. "What the hell. Let's just do it! You're not happy! I'm not happy! What the hell!"

Words I should have said years ago.

I'm laughing, crying, and shouting now.

I can't stop myself.

*Is my mind becoming infected with his disease?*

*Is he making me crazy?*

*This whole thing is crazy!*

My laughter shifts like a switch from shouting to a crazy surge of sobs, retching sobs that rip through my stomach,

heart,

chest,

face,

then to the roots of my hair.

"WHY?" I yell at him.

He slows down the truck.

He's looking for a place to pull over.

"WHY DID YOU TAKE ME AWAY FROM MY CHILDREN? I HATE YOU! YOU SAID YOU CAME HOME TO US! YOU PROMISED **US** A HOME! WHEN YOU MARRIED ME I HAD TWO CHILDREN! YOU MARRIED **US**! YOU PROMISED **US** LOVE AND SAFETY AND THIS IS WHAT YOU GIVE US FOR LOVING YOU? IT GETS A LITTLE TOUGH AND YOU DON'T WANT US ANYMORE? IS THAT WHAT LOVE IS TO YOU?"

My sobs are rasping gasps of pouring rage.

My voice is hoarse from screaming at him.

My head feels like it might explode.

I kick the dashboard.

It feels so good to hit something.

"AND IT WASN'T EVEN TOUGH!" I spew. "YOU made it tough by YOUR OVERCONTROLLING, ANAL RENTENTIVE, IMAGINARY ACCUSTIONS toward an INNOCENT TEENAGER!"

I kick the dashboard again and again and again.

The impact of each blow radiates up my leg but I continue regardless.

This pain numbs the pain I feel in my heart.

My anger geyser blows and I find my voice for another purge. "You don't want THEM, you don't want US and WE; WE are so **DOOOONE**! WHY CAN'T YOU JUST SAY IT? You don't **WANT** A FAMILY ANYMORE, PERIOD! YOU DON'T WANT US ANYMORE SO JUST **LET ME GO**! **MY CHILDREN ARE A PAAAAAART OF ME!** I AM THEIR **MOTHER**! DO YOU NOT GET THAT? I want to go home! I WANT TO GO **HOOOOOOOOOME**! I WANT. To. Go. HOOOOOOOOME!"

I'm gasping for air and the dry sobs are so painful but I accept each one; they numb the worst pain of all: being away from my Children and fearing that I'll be dead before I can tell them what's really been going on here.

They won't know what I've been protecting them from by moving them to their dad's and leaving on this stupid trip.

My patient's face is blank.

He stops the vehicle and gets out.

He comes around to my side of the truck and opens the door.

*Go ahead and throw me out!*

*Leave me on the side of the road!*

*I will walk home!*

He unbuckles me and turns me to face him.

He's tender,
no longer impatient or angry.
"Colleen," he says to me.
I'm so ragged and done.
I close my eyes and then feel his hands on my arms to balance me.
"COLLEEN!" His fingers wipe my tears.
**"COLLEEN!"** He shakes me gently.
I try to open my eyes but they are swollen shut.
"We will go home," James speaks, soothingly. Softly. Kindly. "I'm
sorry. We're going home. I'm sorry. I just can't be with them. I'm
not good for them. I see that. I'm not good for you and I'm not
good for me. I don't know what I'm doing. I don't know what to
do now."
He pulls me to him and holds me.
I feel his arms as simple supports to brace me, not the arms I used
to find refuge within.
Arms hold me while my sobs simmer into crying,
crying calms to scattered breathing,
breathing fades into exhaustion.
Arms turn me back into my seat and buckle me back in,
lay the back rest down,
place a pillow beneath my head,
and cover me with my sweater.
I disappear into my own body.
My spirit curls up into a fetal position around my heart.
He closes the door and checks around the trailer.
He climbs into his seat and we pull back onto the highway,
nice and slow.

# CHAPTER 6

## Missing Puzzle Pieces

"My eyes are finally wide open.
I see where all the missing puzzle pieces fit.
Right there in the spaces
where all the little red flags flew."
– Colleen Songs

Miles and miles of pavement dissolve beneath the wheels.

Two days have gone by since my outburst.

I haven't spoken to him since.

I've been silent as I escape into every passing mile, not putting
any trust in his word to actually get home, but grateful for every
mile closer.

The grey blur of the road erases my presence in the vehicle.

I stay vacant of any thoughts except for those of my Children.

I send them subliminal messages and hope that they capture them.

*I am coming home.*

*I am coming home.*

*I love you so much.*

*You are my strength and my mission.*

*You are my hope and my love made visible.*

*Hope is a powerful tool of survival, my Darlings.*

*It can keep you alive when you have nothing left to support you.*

*I love you.*

*I love you.*

*We will make it better.*

*I will make our lives better.*

*Our love is stronger than this man's hate.*

In my mind, I speak to my parents,

the people who shaped me into me,

the people who will help me to carry on.

*Mom, I need you.*

*Dad, if you can hear me up there, guide me.*

*Guide my Children in my absence.*

I cannot recall when nor where my patient stops for us to rest nor
even if we stop at all.

I slip into autopilot.

Autopilot.

Like the day I moved my Son to his dad's, believing it was better for my boy to grow into his teens with his father.

I was right.

It spared my Son, my gentle giant, the pain of a few tumultuous years with the wrong influence.

My Son wouldn't have been strong enough to take on the storm I sensed was coming.

Autopilot.

Like the day I packed my Daughter's boxes and we drove them to her father's house, only two years after her Brother had been moved there.

As I packed her treasures, my tears flowed into the boxes of her clothes and books.

I missed my family.

I missed the life we once had, the life that was dismantled one piece of us at a time.

Autopilot.

Like the day he drove me away from my Children.

I saw them in the front window of their dad's house, waving.

Waving tearful goodbyes to me from their father's home,

a home without me.

I could feel their confused and shattered hearts.

The sight flipped a switch in me and I felt a surge of panic in my brain like a circuit rush!

Panic that I would never see them again,

panic that I had lost them forever;

the first of many panic attacks to come.

I craned my neck for as long as I could to see my Children:

wanting to tell them they were safer there,

wanting to tell them that Momma just needed to sort this out.

I pled with God to not let them feel abandoned.

Meanwhile, James assured me this was the best thing for everyone.

*Asshole!*

His words were dead to my ears, and as I lost sight of my Children,
I felt my lifeline being severed with every mile between us.
He kept driving.
I don't remember breathing, or eating, or sleeping for weeks after
my last sight of my Children.
Autopilot.

Miles keep rolling by.
Day three.
Lost in my thoughts to escape from his presence.
I had been brought up believing that abuse was a wife being
beaten or cheated on, a trusted friend or in-law molesting my older
siblings, a sister kicked out of the house by the rage of alcohol in
their husbands' veins seemed terribly wrong too.
Being yelled at, belittled, and kept in the kitchen didn't seem
right either.
I was the youngest.
As a child, I don't think they thought I understood that things
were wrong.
But I did.
Children know.
They have the most honest feelings of right and wrong.
I question this definition of abuse today.
There's so much more to abuse.
As memories file through my head like a movie reel, I recall some
of the little red flags that tweaked my gut; things that didn't add up
from early on.
At the time I trusted his tearful, begging excuses due to his lack of
knowing "how to love" from growing up in an abusive home:
the beatings,
the booze,
the cheating.

The signs of abuse James showed me were not ones I was famil-
iar with.

Although he never actually lifted a hand to me,

he opened his mouth over and over again,

threw things,

accused me of cheating,

and called me a 'mental' c-word more than once.

He liked that word as it was his ultimate, degrading curse
of choice.

His words and calculated motions of isolation and emotional depri-
vation were his most cunning personal weapons of choice.

I force my mind to pull back the fog and begin to question everything.

Has he been slowly dismantling my life in order to control it: the
narcissist's signature tactic?

Is he really sick or is he simply narcissistic?

Is it one and the same?

*Red flags.*

The wisdom within that warns you to feel that something is wrong.

My mind starts sliding through time as fast as the trees passing
outside my window.

As we blankly proceed through the Canadian/U.S. border,

questions pop up that I've wanted to ask but have either denied
or doubted.

Little red flags.

Courage sweeps over me.

*What the heck.*

*What have I got to lose now?*

*I'm going for it.*

"Remember that time when we were about a month into formally
dating?" I ask, my voice weak from my three-day span of silence.

"We had planned to spend the evening together but you called to cancel. You told me you just wanted to stay home and watch a movie and have time to not think about anything."

The memory is so clear I feel like I'm there again.

I turn to look at him.

"I asked if you wanted to talk instead. We hadn't spoken to each other nor seen each other for a few days and we usually liked to get together to talk. It was so unlike you. You said no, that you wanted to stay home and watch a movie. You seemed really rushed to get off the phone."

He is flushed.

He looks out the window.

*He remembers.*

I look out my window.

*I knew it.*

"We were just dating then, Colleen," he hisses. "You know that! Why are you talking about that? What's the point? Let things go. We're done, I get it."

"Who was it?" I push him further. "We have nothing to hold on to anymore. Let's clean the slate now so we can heal faster later."

The road leads towards home, making me feel brave in this moment of finding the missing puzzle pieces and foggy bits that have clouded my judgement all this time.

"She was in my AA group," he finally admits. "She called me and said she needed someone to talk to and her sponsor wasn't listening."

He's aggravated but resolute.

*That's all I get?*

I want to push for more details, even though his answers have already started my stomach churning; I am so angry with myself that I didn't call him out on it back then.

Another red flag moment pops into my mind.

We had a booming gas station and carwash in Pearson, favoured among the community, but darkened by a looming lawsuit with the

previous owners that kept him stressed and held him back from
making it what he imagined it could be.

He needed regular breaks and holidays away to help him cope.
I remember another holiday he went on by himself, a didgeridoo
retreat at the same place he had gone to with Rob.

He seemed to favour that place, and this time he went alone.

"Your first didgeridoo lesson retreat?" I question. "You went on
your own that time and I stayed to watch the business."

I urge him to remember what I could never quite forget. "The first
night after you had your first lesson you called to ask me if your
body looked okay and if I could tell that you worked out? You said
you were invited to the hot tub with the group."

Over the phone later that night he said that the group was somewhere else.

I didn't think anything of it at the time.

Maybe I misunderstood?

People's plans change.

I breathe into my belly to try and stop the tension that's starting to
creep up in anticipation of his reply.

*You are asking for clarity.*

*Well, prepare yourself.*

*It is all coming to light now.*

He takes his time.

He's quiet.

He moves around in his seat, agitated, but he doesn't speed up
the truck.

"We didn't kiss," he admits. "No one was there, Colleen; just this
girl I knew you'd never meet. We went to the beach and played our
didj and fooled around but we never kissed."

He looks over at me as though he's trying to reassure me it was
okay to just 'fool around' when you have a girlfriend at home.

I look at him in disbelief then turn away.

He knows what I'm thinking.

49

*Seriously?*

*Oh well, as long as you didn't kiss.*

*Heaven knows how long it has been since you have kissed me.*

"What about Tallahassee?" I ask. "When you went to the franchise training course?"

I remember his phone call to me that night too, asking if this shirt went with that pair of pants, and if I thought he was too old to go out clubbing with the group to celebrate the successful end of the course.

I had told him to relax and be happy about his accomplishments with his new friends and that it meant a better business for us.

Then, when he came home, I found a woman's business card. Inscribed on the back were the words "All good things must come to an end," hearts, and a home phone number.

When I first approached him with the woman's business card, he said he had wanted to remember the song they had all heard that night.

He told me it was their group song and it was supposed to remind them of all the fun they had – that was what the note meant.

He said I was overreacting and then walked away from me.

This time his hesitation spans longer.

"Janelle was her name," I remind him. "Ja. Nelle. A pretty name. Was she pretty? Did you have fun that night? What did you do? You never did share that with me; you always changed the subject."

I casually put my sweater over my body and wrap my arms around my stomach.

I need protection,

comfort,

courage.

My sweater is warm and soft to the touch, unlike the hard-hearted man sitting next to me.

"We just danced at the club, all right?" he explodes. "She was afraid to fly and had to leave early that next morning. Her roommate was already gone and she didn't want to stay in her room alone. She shared my room that night and I took her to the airport. Happy now, Colleen? Really? You know, your jealously has always turned me off."

*There it is.*

*That blame-turning, condescending excuse he has used so many times before.*

*Can he not hear himself?*

*He truly believes he was justified to cheat and lie.*

I look over at him in complete amusement.

It's not funny but my feelings are all jumbled up.

Bewildered.

Betrayed.

Defiled.

Foolish.

Sad.

Hurt.

Angry.

I start to feel the colour rise in my cheeks as anger wins over the others.

*Here we go again!*

"She was afraid to fly but had no trouble flying there in the first place?" I softly begin my own condescending rage. "She didn't want to stay in her room alone? What? Was she six years old? Oh My Goodness! How the fuck did she get there in the first place?" I laugh and continue, sarcasm drenching every word. "You were so thoughtful to let her stay with you and share your room and not tell your wife for fear of her misunderstanding and being all jealous. Wow! You are so kind to spare me that!"

I'm laughing again.

His stories are comical.

Stupidly comical.

My blind trust in him even more so.

"All good things must come to an end, indeed," I say.

My anger gives way to fury.

I'm livid!

Not at him, though:

at myself,

for being so naïve,

so trusting;

for taking care of the business at home so many times
in good faith.

He was doing things that made him happy while I made the best of
it; trying to support my husband.

He got the breaks he needed from having his own business twenty-
four/seven and I toiled to make everything work between the
business, home, school, the Children, and a split family.

*He got his breaks alright… and affairs to feed his what?*

*WHAT?*

*His ego?*

*His sick brain?*

*How did I miss all of these signs?*

He says nothing.

His face is red.

He lights a cigarette and opens the window.

I'm growing hotter with every awakening thought.

I'm trying to comprehend what it all means.

"You mean to tell me those times when **I** juggled the Children,
their school, the home, the business, their days with their own
father, all for **YOU** to have a break, you were 'fooling around'?"
I ask. "Those times when the Children pitched in and helped
out and spent extra hours helping me at home, helping me at
work, while **YOU** went away because you were stressed, you were
fooling around?"

Rage!

"Those times when they'd plan a welcome home dinner or surprise for you, you were FOOOOLING AROUND and saw NOTHING wrong with it?"

My blood is lava!

It boils up from my feet to my brain.

"I'm furious! **I'm so bloody furious!** YOU CALL MY CHILDREN SELFISH AND UNGRATEFUL, ARE YOU KIDDING ME? You didn't touch me for months, and then YEARS, blaming it on stress, and you were fooling around with other women and thinking that was fine and well, AS LONG AS YOU DIDN'T KISS!!! You wonder why I got JEALOUS? ALL THIS TIME! Please, please, tell me… WHY DIDN'T YOU JUST FUCKING LEAVE?"

No response from him other than throwing his cigarette out the window.

I pray it's out before hitting the grass on the side of the road.

*Always, and only thinking of yourself.*

*Now set a fire out there, why don't you!*

Then he opens his mouth and blurts out excuses.

"I DIDN'T WANT TO TOUCH YOU BECAUSE I HAD BEEN WITH THOSE OTHER WOMEN, Colleen! Listen to yourself," he yells, frustrated that I can't see his reasoning. "DON'T YOU GET IT?" he shouts at me. "You, **YOU,** made it SO EASY for me to take advantage of you!"

His voice is filled with disgust.

He's gripping the steering wheel so tightly that his knuckles are white.

I am speechless.

My eyes are finally wide open.

I see where all the missing puzzle pieces fit.

Right there in the spaces

where all the little red flags flew.

# CHAPTER 7

## Georgian Bay

"I lie in the sand
and hear the song of the geese and ducks
as they fly above the water
then softly land to float."
– Colleen Songs

My thoughts race through the path of flags that led me to
this moment.
My guts twist from the insanity of the man who sits beside me.
I curl up in the seat of the truck and let the painted lines of the
highway pull me home.
*Just take me home,*
*out of this nightmare!*
His words, the words of someone who was once my husband, cut
me deeply.
His confessions leave me confused and ashamed, stripped
and used.
I'm reeling from the flashing memories and signs that I
couldn't see.
*I was so blind!*
*I should have been aware of what was going on!*
I plea to God, or whoever the hell He or She or It is; that mysteri-
ous something that we innately lean on when life seems stupidly
out of whack.
*Why wasn't I made aware of the cheating at the time?*
*Everyone would have understood why I had to leave him!*
*All this time, all this effort, and I was never even really wanted!*
*My kids and I were a convenience.*
*We were the image of the happy family he merely wanted to possess.*
I wrap my arms tighter around my waist for fear of my body burst-
ing from the anger welling up inside my core.
My elbows sit uncomfortably on my protruding hip bones.
I've lost so much weight I can feel my frame beneath my skin.
*I am wasting away!*
*What have I allowed this man to do to me?*
*Why did I let him take me away from my Children?*
*What a fool I am!*
*What a naïve and stupid fool I am for believing all of his lies and*
*empty promises!*

We finally stop at a campground on Georgian Bay, Lake
Huron, Ontario.
No longer on autopilot.
I am wide awake.
I just want out of the truck.
From days of driving and roadside stops we're both exhausted and
I'm emotionally beaten.
I need to be away from breathing the same air as him but I help set
up the RV in memorized silence.
I'm so glad to be back on Canadian soil.
I want so badly to reach out and see if any of my many distant
relatives live in the area.
I want to ask them to come and take me away from this
wretched situation.
But I'm ashamed of my life and my choices and hobbled by the
certain uncertainty of his reaction if I try and reach out to anyone.
I cannot even if I wanted to.
He keeps the phone at all times.
I gather a towel and my bathing suit and head towards the water.
*The water will cool my boiling mind and dampen the fire in my body.*
*Otherwise, I will be so close to the edge of reason that I might not make it back.*
*I just need to be by the water.*
He doesn't bother following me.
With every step forward to the lake I feel guided.
I have no idea where I'm going.
I'm just going.
I smell campfire and see the colours of beach towels and
bathing suits hanging on makeshift clotheslines which decorate
the pathways.
I hear the surf of the water getting closer.
I follow the rhythmic lure until I arrive at the shoreline:
a little piece of paradise.

Short shrubs and grass peek out here and there from a carpet of
sand and driftwood.
Small cabins and camper vans are hidden behind groomed bushes
dividing each individual oasis.
I find a little cove of sand with random pieces of driftwood
slumbering amidst tall wisps of grass.
The sun is hot and the waves are soft.
I lie in the sand and hear the song of the geese and ducks as they
fly above the water then softly land to float.
There is no one else on the beach.
Just me.
*Thank you, whoever you are in that big blue sky.*
I let the tears spill like bile: ugly, vile, and bitter.
All this time,
all the nights I cried myself to sleep,
all the effort to understand,
to accept,
to adjust.
All the lies that he was just sick,
stressed,
that he didn't know what love was;
all that time he was seeing other women!
*He could touch them and please them and himself but he could not touch me?*
*Instead he blames me?*
*Why did he ever want to marry me when every night he would flinch from even*
*a kiss goodnight?*
*Why did I stay?*
I look around to be sure I'm alone on the beach and then I take off
my clothes and put on my bathing suit.
I'm past the point of caring about propriety.
It has done nothing to serve me in return.
Decency.
Kindness.

Trust.

Vows.

*It's all bull shit!*

I join the gulls in the water and let the waves move me.

The motion allows for more tears to well up and be released.

*My Children,*

*I am sorry.*

*I am sorry I let this happen to us.*

*How could I let this happen to us?*

*I wish you were here with me instead.*

*I wish I had kept our life for just us.*

*I can hear your voices in my mind and I miss you both.*

*I am coming home.*

*There is no hope for him.*

*He does not want us.*

*He never did.*

*He used us.*

*I am so sorry.*

I close my eyes.

I listen to the seagulls and let the waves cradle me until I'm too
chilly to stay in the water.

I get out,

wrap myself up in my towel,

sit on the beach,

and watch the birds swim.

The stillness is calming and I feel myself recharging.

I lay down to sink into the warm soft sand, close my eyes

and breathe.

Suddenly I'm cold.

I sense someone close by.

I've fallen asleep and it's now dusk.

I sit up from my sandy bed and see him sitting beside me.

He has his cell phone.

"You should really call your son and tell him we're back in Canada," James offers, nervously juggling the phone in his hands.

Left to right.

Right to left.

"But don't talk to Sissy," he warns, raising his opposite hand to point a scolding finger. "I'll know if you do. Until she tells me she's sorry, you're not allowed to speak to her. Don't you dare cave like you always do, Colleen. She'll never learn."

I know he's only offering me the phone because it has been a while since anyone from my family knew where we were.

He hands me the phone.

I take it eagerly.

I call my Son.

# CHAPTER 8

## Let My Daughter Go!

"Let my Daughter go!
LET MY DAUGHTER GO!
LET MY DAUGHTER GO!"
– Colleen Songs

The phone rings,

and rings.

I press the sound of it harder against my ear.

I do not want to share a whisper with James who looms above me,
hanging on my every breath.

I fear this call won't be answered when the receiver sees it's me.

"Hello," comes a deep, humble voice over the line.

*His voice is changing!*

"Andrew! Andrew, it's Mom!" my voice cracks from the bliss
of hearing his voice. "Oh, my Sonshine! I can finally call you.
Reception is very difficult here," I lie.

I pray he can read my heart.

He usually can.

When eye-to-eye we seem to be able to sense one another's thoughts.

I curse myself for not trusting in this gift a long time ago.

"Oh yeah. Where are you now, Mom?" he asks in an effort to
sound happy, interested, genuine.

He's making the most of it like we've been programmed to do.

His voice!

My Sonshine!

My heart aches with a pain that reaches my backbone.

I bite my lip to stop the tears.

"We just got back to Canada," I say. "I'm at Georgian Bay on Lake
Huron. It's so pretty here. We'll have to come one day."

*Do not cry.*

*Do not cry.*

*DO NOT CRY!*

"The lake is like an ocean and it's so warm," I add. "Nothing is fun
without you guys though."

I shoot a glance at my patient as he shakes his head at me, triggered
by my 'babying', as he would call it.

I almost dare him to react.

I have the phone now.

One word is all I need to say.

Help!

One word would tell them this is all a lie.

I might not make it back alive after I utter it, but then they would know the truth.

James has surpassed his tolerance of allowing me this phone call.

I can tell by the increasing redness of his face.

Testing him this blatantly would send him over the edge.

I block him out of my thoughts as I focus on my Son.

We chat about everyday things and I close my eyes to imagine him close to me.

I recollect his musky boy scent and his soft thick hair.

I imagine kissing his head, breathing him in.

*Absorb every word.*

*Be in our happy moment right past the very last second.*

"Well," he says.

He's wrapping up the conversation.

I feel the same wave of panic that I felt when we pulled away from the Children as they waved from the window of their father's house.

Tears creep into my voice.

I don't want to let him go.

"Where are you going to be, Mom?" he inquires in his new young man's voice.

His undertone asks a deeper question than his words.

I hear it.

*I hear you.*

*I know what you are asking.*

I want to tell him that I'm coming home but I remain shackled by the entity hovering over me.

"We're on our way back west, darling. I'll call you when I get to Medicine Hat, okay?"

I try to reassure him.

He mostly keeps his feelings to himself, but he has seen and heard things happen.

He saw his Sister come to his Dad's so stressed during spring break.

He heard things over the phone.

He witnessed her tears and confusion.

Thankfully, his soft heart knew only a portion of the turmoil Sissy and I endured.

*Do I ask if Sissy is okay?*

*If she wants to talk?*

My patient is already pacing, agitated, daring me to cross the line and ask about Sissy.

I have a clever thought and hope my Son will catch on.

"Have either of you heard how Mummu is doing?" I enquire.

Taking a chance.

Mummu is my Mom, my kids' Finnish-Canadian Grandma.

From the time they could talk they called her Mummu.

"I know she likes to talk to you and your sister," I continue, keeping a close watch on James' reaction. "She could use a phone call to let her know I am fine. Could you do that for me?"

My Mother.

The Children are close to her.

If anyone could read their saddened hearts, it would be Mom.

If anyone could reassure them, it would be Mom.

I have not told her the real reason why the Children are now with their father and we are away.

She would want to fix it and thus be in harm's way.

I feel what she is thinking though.

Every day.

But I also feel that she would suspect that there is something more to this for me to leave my Children for so long.

The truth will come out when I know everyone is safe from him.

If anyone could let my Children know their Mother loves them, it would be my Mom. She would plant the seed of, "That's not like your Mom; something's not right for your Momma to be away from you."

"Okay, Mom. Sure I will," my Son promises me.

We say "I love you" and I let the call end.

My hearing shifts back to the waves,

to my breath.

I don't want to let go of the fading resonance of my Son's voice.

I hold onto the phone until James reaches out to take it from me.

"Did he even ask how I was?" James disappears and I succumb to my patient's question. "Probably not, considering the selfish, ungrateful kids you have."

Same old things he says whenever anyone is happy.

*He can twist an orange into a lemon!*

*If it's not about him, it's against him.*

*No one can have a moment's peace and love.*

*Not one fucking moment!*

I rub my temples to soothe the ache his mindless words cause me.

He drags on a newly lit cigarette before speaking again. "I sent an e-mail to Wayne."

My heart squeezes in my chest as he speaks.

"What! Why? What did you say now?" My temper rises as I stand to face him.

*God!*

*Can I not have a moment to savour my conversation with my Son?*

*Can I not drown this evil entity?*

*PLEASE?*

I startle myself with this request to my Maker to drown the man in front of me.

I madly gather my things.

"WHAT. DID. YOU. SAY?" I demand through gritted teeth.

"I had to let him know the kind of father he is," my patient spits out, stepping forward to eliminate any distance between us. "I had to let him know what we need him to do if we are to have any hope for your kids, Colleen!"

I push him away from me.

"DO you not GET it?" he pokes me in the forehead. "Does your stupid, mental brain not GET it? Your slut of a daughter…"

I throw my things at him and lunge like a leopard threatening its kill.

I'm beyond my temper.

I LOOOOATHE this man!

"DON'T YOU EVER CALL MY DAUGHTER THAT! SHE ISN'T A SLUT! SHE'S A NORMAL TEEN WHO HAD HER FIRST NORMAL, INNOCENT RELATIONSHIP AND YOU COULDN'T STAY OUT OF IT!"

I'm so close to his face that he cringes.

He looks into my eyes, shocked that I could react so viciously.

He's never seen me in this claw-drawn state and I rejoice that I have it in me to give.

"WHEN YOU WERE SIXTEEN DID YOU NOT HAVE A CRUSH?" I ask. "DID YOU NOT SNEAK AROUND? DID YOU NOT TELL YOUR PARENTS WHERE YOU WERE?"

I can smell his breath, rancid from the cigarettes, and I want to puke.

"It wasn't a crush, Colleen! Are you that stupid?" he comes at me. "She would have run away! She would have let him touch her!" He tries to grab my arm and I stagger backwards.

"YOU ARE INSANE! YOU ARE TWISTED! SHE NEVER DID ANYTHING! DID **YOU** HAVE PERMISSION FROM EVERY ONE OF **YOUR** GIRLFRIENDS' FATHERS TO SCREW THEM?" I want to claw his face off! "When YOU were sixteen YOU'D ALREADY HAD A THIRTEEN-YEAR-OLD! DID YOU ASK FIRST? DID YOU TELL HER FATHER YOU

WERE GOING TO SCREW HIS DAUGHTER IN YOUR
CAR? DID YOU GET HIS BLESSING? DID YOU CALL HER
A SLUT?"

I hit his chest.

That feels good.

"MY DAUGHTER DIDN'T DOOOOO ANYTHING like
THAT!" I hit his chest with every other word. "SHE. WAS.
INNOCENT! HE WAS A NICE BOY! THEY WOULD HAVE
LIVED AND LEARNED!"

My voice is breaking, my face is burning hot, and my fingers are
clenched so tightly into my palms that my nails dig into my skin
with every punch to his chest.

*You are insane!*

*I am going to drown you,*

*get in the truck,*

*and drive the fuck home!*

This thought feels almost normal.

*Anyone would understand!*

I feel a degree of relief at the thought.

It was enough to get me to turn away and leave him there, still
breathing his wasted breath.

I hurry back to the RV and lock the door.

*God get me through this!*

*Get me home.*

*Get me closer to my family.*

*You have GOT to step in here!*

*Please let Wayne know it was not me writing to him!*

*Please let my Children call Mom so a hint of love can be given from me through
their contact with her.*

*And get me home before I kill him!*

*He is so far gone he is insane, and he is making me insane along with him.*

I fall to my knees.

The thought of harming another human scares me.

On my knees, I weep into the carpet.

Memories of the day he wouldn't let Sissy leave the house after humiliating her at school.

He held her down as she fought with him to leave her alone.

I was so afraid of what he'd do next.

I asked him to let my Daughter go!

Let my Daughter go!

She cried.

We fought.

Her eyes bore into me for help.

For protection.

I was afraid to push him further for fear he'd crush her.

I called her dad on the phone to try and calm her down so that James would let her go.

He would think James was crazy and come get us out of this mess.

But he couldn't see it through the phone.

I was alone pleading.

Let my Daughter go!

LET MY DAUGHTER GO!

LET MY DAUGHTER GO!

# CHAPTER 9

## Rippled Panes

"I smiled through held-back tears,
angry with his words,
waving to them through the rippled panes
of the porch windows."
– Colleen Songs

Our exchange of words is left to poison the sandy beaches of
Lake Erie.
I feel drained,
exhausted,
void of any belief that there would be any escape from this tyrant.
He never sticks to his word.
He only promises things to get his way.
*What did I ever see in him?*
*Why can I not get away?*
*Why did this have to happen to my beautiful Children and me?*
*They have only ever done their best!*
*They are Children!*
*Why did I bring him into our lives?*
The lines on the road blur.
Signs fly by like the flapping wings of a circling bird,
hovering over its prey,
waiting for the weakest moment to dive,
to aim,
to kill.
We're coming up to the little Saskatchewan town where we lived
before leaving on this journey.

Only four hours away from Andrew meant easy travelling on
weekends and holidays.
Sissy and I loved this little town that took us in as though we had
always belonged there.
We were enchanted by the tumbling sage brush, the aroma of
bakery-fresh bread wafting through town, the vintage red velvet
theatre ran by the Kinettes, and the 'real' art teacher who was
amazed with Sissy's artistic abilities.
A family took her under their wing and taught her the beloved
horsemanship that she ached to learn.
She was a natural.

She spent every day at the ranch tending to her own horse, her birthday gift from us, until the tragic day my patient took Sissy's horse away from her.

My gut can't take seeing the town again as we drive closer, but my heart wants to catch every detail.
I **have** *to see it one more time.*
*There it is!*

The abandoned grain tower that I imagined remodelling as a home and bed and breakfast.
Our adorable little ranch house with the lead panes of glass surrounding the enclosed porch.
The haunted swing chair that began to swing on its own one warm, winter afternoon.
The plaid-clothed ghost arms that Sissy swore she felt around her.
We were told he was one of the original owners; a gentle soul and proud father of many daughters.
He had loved the house they lived in and didn't want to leave.
The scent of peppermint enfolded my Daughter as those plaid arms took my place, holding her as she cried and cried in her room.
And me,
captured in a desperate fog,
trying to make everything okay.

Tears fall as I feel every memory slide by:
the noon hour alarm from town hall,
the train whistling as it passed by,
the ladies in the post office who knew me by name.
One of them bought my bicycle when we left.
I remember the nervous young man joining Sissy for lunch at our house, his spoon shaking with every mouthful.

I had tried to make him feel comfortable, but James' jibes across the table stabbed the boy's innocence like a blade.

I watched my Daughter and this boy walk back to school, laughing and talking.

I thought how sweet it was.

But James interpreted their attraction as 'dirty' by his accusations and over-protectiveness.

I smiled through held-back tears, angry with the words he spewed behind their backs, waving to the kids through the rippled panes of the porch windows.

*Rippled panes.*
*How symbolic of our life.*
*Not smooth and accepting,*
*but marred, uneven, and always in pain.*
*Distorted reality.*
*Rippled panes.*
I sit back in my seat.

I can no longer see the little town.

I pray the people know that the woman they met was not the real me.

She was the blind me.

I pray for forgiveness from the young man my patient splintered with his accusations.

I vow to call him one day and ask his forgiveness.

I pray the town saw past my excuses for this man's actions as I attempted to make a good life for my family.

I glance over at him as he drives.

He's quiet and his jaw is set.

*Is he disturbed from passing by the town that made his personality and*
*illness visible?*
*Visible to himself, to us, to the public?*

*Does he recall making a scene in the school parking lot, screaming at my*
*Daughter and her friend?*
*Does he remember calling me a mental bitch in front of everyone in the bar that*
*night when I tried to get him to come home so that he wouldn't drink and drive?*

I cried,
standing there in the bar,
like a fool.
I tore off my wedding rings in my embarrassed fury,
laid them beside his pack of cigarettes,
told him I couldn't live this way anymore.
He threw them at me as I made my way out the door.
They hit my head like bullets and clunked to the floor at my feet.
Out-of-control visibility!
Even the woman nestled up to him felt badly for me.
She helped me pick up my rings and hesitated before returning to
her drink beside him.

After all the confessions of affairs and other women before he was
sick, a time when I had thought things were going well, I try to
recall a moment when I felt he loved me.
*When was the last time he touched me intimately, even with a hug or a kiss?*
I used to know.
With a busy life running a business and me running the family and
home, it used to be easy to remember the day and time with blush-
ing sentimentality, but as weeks passed, then months, then years,
the last time had become a forgotten, past-life experience.
The road pulls us into his Alberta hometown.
We park the RV at the golf course campground and set it up, again
in silence.
*Oh, the balm of silence!*
I pack my things for the night.

We agree I will stay with his mother while we sort out our next steps of separation and my return home.

He insists.

He doesn't want to leave me with the RV.

He has become very territorial of it now that we have agreed to end our marriage, even though he speaks as though we are still 'we'.

I don't care.

I simply want a real bed for a night.

She's happy to see us.

She hugs us, and makes his favourite dinner of homemade noodles.

We eat supper with her and her lovely, aging Aunt.

I like her Aunt.

I like her elegance and witty humour.

I try to stay cheery though I know this will probably be my last friendly supper with these ladies.

His mother and I have a good relationship, but I know blood is thicker than water.

I am very aware that she will listen to his instructions about how to control me while I am there.

And they will come.

I shrug it off.

To stay overnight somewhere completely away from him is worth rattling a few more chains.

I no longer want to wake up in the same place as him anyway, even if we haven't shared the same bed in months.

I clear the supper dishes as everyone chats.

I shower and get myself ready for bed.

A bed!

From the day of his confession, I've been sleeping on the sofa bed in the RV's living room.

He wouldn't let me have the bedroom to myself even when I shut the door.

He is 'king', you know.

"You know I need a bed, Colleen. You know I need a good sleep."
His excuses justify his lack of chivalry.
It is **his** bed and **his** money and **his...his...his**.
I don't want to fight anymore, nor do I want lay beside him
ever again.
So I have been sleeping on the sofa bed despite his long hours of
rocking in his chair, sipping his vodka, and flicking channels.
Life
is only
about
him.


I have met a few people with mental illness and addictions over
the years:
alcohol addiction,
pharmaceutical addiction,
bipolar disorder,
manic depression,
depression,
seasonal depression,
postpartum depression.
Heck I've had bouts of depression myself;
I think we all do at some points in our lives.
Life isn't easy.
I have met some who are so sweetly and earnestly practicing
everything they can to be well.
They still value their life and don't want to miss it.
They value the lives of others and respect their place in their loved
one's lives with a sense of responsibility.
Others use their plight as an excuse to continue with their behav-
ioural patterns, no matter who they hurt.
The latter is my patient.
Confused, I asked for help.

Help, because it was so hard to live like this.
I was met with judgmental comments from nurses, doctors,
and counsellors:
"You wouldn't leave your husband if he had cancer, would you?"
"Is mental illness an excuse to leave your spouse? He wasn't always
this way."
They'd look down at their papers,
writing notes,
aware of my unawareness,
with me very much aware of how unaware they were of me.
I went to them hoping for clarity, for education about what I was
dealing with.
I left feeling embarrassed and ashamed for asking for help when he
was the one with the illness.
Why did we take this trip, without doctor's knowledge or approval,
only months after my patient was diagnosed with a severe
mental illness?
Hope, I guess.
Scrambling fear?
I no longer recall.
I was simply desperate for something,
anything,
to change.


Leaving the bathroom after preparing myself for bed, I hear
talking in the kitchen.
As I enter the little room, I hear him saying how the kids have
ruined us and they've given us no choice.
*He has told his mother we are over but not the truth of why.*
I look over at his mother at the little kitchen table.
She reveals her concern with hunched shoulders and hands wrung
around her coffee cup.
She tells him that it's probably for the best.

I see their notepads and lists,

numbers and financial calculations.

They stop talking when they notice I'm in the room.

*Bankers!*

*Always thinking about the bottom line and how to cover their asses.*

*I am not even cold and they are figuring out how to shut me up and cut me out.*

*Do not worry about your stinking money;*

*I only asked for your love in return for mine.*

I make myself a tea, my back towards them, so he can't read my

irritated expression.

With my freedom just around the corner I don't care what

they're concocting.

*The courts will decide.*

*I will focus on my future!*

*Who knows what he said to her while I was showering, probably whatever was*

*in his imagination to exonerate himself from any blame.*

I sip my tea and take a deep, cleansing breath.

It's time to set things in motion.

By the knots in my belly I fear this isn't going to be an

easy getaway.

I lean against the kitchen counter and take another sip, going over

the plan in my head.

I have two options.

The first is to just leave,

call the Children's dad,

and ask him to come and get me.

But I know that option will expose them to several more acts of

abuse from my patient.

The thought of Wayne and my Children undergoing any

further threats,

foul language,

stalking,

vicious e-mails,

terrifying phone calls,

any further dis-ease than they have already endured

makes my decision for me:

Option two.

*What's my option two?*

And as I'm about to panic a light flickers on!

*Jayne!*

*This could work!*

I take another sip as I scan scenarios that are now spilling through my mind.

My girlfriend Jayne lives in Northern British Columbia.

She's pregnant and abandoned by her fiancé who "changed his mind" about wanting a family.

Jayne is well into her second trimester by now, approaching her third.

"How could I let her have this baby all by herself?" I asked my patient when we received her news one night several months ago.

She called to say her Mr. Right was Mr. I'm-Not-Ready-To-Be-Dad, so he beat her and threw her out.

She knew that she had to go home to her family in Oregon so that she and the baby would have family to help them.

She had decided to put her beautiful little homestead in Quesnel, B.C. up for sale.

And she wanted me to be with her when baby was due.

James was sincerely concerned about her at that time and had promised both her and me that we would be there.

*I need to know her status!*

*We may have agreed to end our marriage, but I don't trust him.*

*He still holds me hostage with the volatility of his reaction to anything that threatens his control, and the thought of my returning to my Children.*

*I need to make plans to go to her "temporarily," and simply not return.*

*He knows that I am a new-baby-aholic so he won't expect me back for a few months depending on her status.*

*It is the perfect plan, already set in motion by our earlier agreement to help Jayne when baby comes.*

*In his mind, it will take me away from my Children that much longer and give him time to plot whatever it is he is plotting.*

*Divorce?*

*Oh, he's going to be brutal over a divorce, but I'll surprise him by not fighting him.*

*I won't ask for anything but my own personal things.*

*I can make it on my own without him.*

*I'd rather!*

*He'll never go away if we have ties like his precious money still looming between us.*

*For now, I will leave all my precious things behind, even my treasured guitar, and just take what I need.*

*I never go anywhere without my guitar.*

*He'll think I will return if I leave her behind.*

*Beautiful guitar, you've got my back, like so many times before.*

"I'd like to call Jayne and see how she's doing," I say, interrupting the conversation between mother and son.

Knowing he has to keep looking innocent in front of his mother, he pulls out a chair and hands me his phone – his signal that he wants to hear what I'm saying.

I sit down and take the phone.

My lack of trust is now justified.

*Think what you want.*

*Jayne will just 'know' what I am doing anyway.*

I silently giggle to myself.

*Every time I've actually been able to see Jayne has been when either she or I have had man trouble.*

I set my psyche up to transmit this intention into my call to her as I dial her number.

"Hi!" comes her voice.

Cheery as ever.

"Oh, my gosh! Where are you now?" she asks.

"We're back at my mother-in-law's. You remember Rose?" I reply, overdoing it a little with my own cheer. "It's been a long trip. Nice to be back. How are you? How's Baby coming along?"

We chat and chat and catch up on each other's lives.

She is not due until November.

Three months to go.

*It's the perfect time for me to come and help her sell, pack, and move before the baby is born!*

I can tell both my patient and his mother are annoyed with my cheeriness.

Coffee keeps getting topped up.

My patient keeps tapping his pen on the table.

They want to keep talking about their plan to get rid of me quietly and protect their money, I assume.

*Oh well!*

*You want to spy on my conversations, I'm going to talk all I want.*

I quickly scan the list on the table.

I notice task entries like 'change will', 'kids out', 'add sister'.

He catches me looking at the paper and flips the list over.

I just look at him.

*Mother Fucker!*

*The kids only wanted your love!*

I refocus on my friend's update.

**My plan** and **friend** deserve my full attention.

I tell her once again that we don't want her to be alone when baby comes.

I emphasize 'we'.

She asks me about the Children and I continue on without mentioning them.

"All is as good as it can be," I fib through my cheerfulness. "Now that we're back in Medicine Hat I am thinking it would be the perfect time for me to come and stay with you for a while. I can

help you sell the property, move back to Oregon, and be with you
when the baby comes."

I look over at James and smile.

He doesn't return my smile but his face carries a thoughtful expression.

My heart drops a little.

*What are you thinking now?*

Her reply is a simple throaty laugh.

*Please, Jayne, know what I am saying!*

"It'll be perfect, Jayne. You've always been there for me. It's
my turn."

*This would be perfect.*

After a few moments of excited chatter, she agrees to call as soon
as she can get everything arranged.

She asks to talk to my patient.

*God, Jayne, you are brilliant!*

I hand him the phone.

She tells him how excited she is for my visit and how much
she appreciates him.

She tells him that her Mom is a travel agent, so if he pays for
my airfare to fly to Prince George, BC, the nearest airport to
Quesnel, she will book and pay for my airfare back from Oregon
when everything is settled and I've had my fill of 'new baby' time.

He agrees.

By the pleased look on his face, he is evidently delighted
with himself.

He ends the call.

"Thank you," I express to him. "It'll be nice to see her and her
Baby. No one should be alone when they have their baby, and I
can't imagine prepping property for sale and moving an entire
farm when you're pregnant."

His mother agrees with me and we chit chat pleasantly for a minute
or two, my angst dissipating through the light conversation.

I have missed her.

It will hurt a little to lose her.

"Well, I'm off to sleep," I say. "See you in the morning."

I take my leave and go to the room that will embrace me through my first night of freedom.

But before I reach the bedroom door I hear his voice:

"We must watch Colleen, Mom. No calls to anyone. I trust Jayne. See how **she** gets it by asking **me** to make the arrangements to get Colleen there? She gets it! She's always been good to me."

I hear his coffee cup hit the table hard.

"You have to tell me if Colleen tries to call anyone else. She'll try and reach the kids and they're not getting a thing from me. I'm nothing to them, and if you let her call them, then I am nothing to you."

I hear his chair scrape on the floor.

I hear his footsteps up the stairway to the door.

I hear the door open, then a few more muffled words between them.

I hear the door close.

I hear Rose's slippered footsteps and light switches snapping off.

I sleep.

# CHAPTER 10

## "Tough beans on him!"

"Just the thought of Her
gives me more courage and determination
to begin my journey
back to myself,
my Children,
and my life.
– Colleen Songs

For a few minutes, I'm not sure where I am.

I see the light from the window and know that it's morning.

I look around and realize that I'm in my mother-in-law's
spare bedroom.

I recognize my own Mother's set of dressers that my patient had
purchased when my family had to move her to an assisted living
home in Kelowna.

Then I remember where I am.

My Mother's dressers warm me and my memories of her give
me courage.

Memories that make me smile as I think of the fun we had while
she lived with me and my Children after Dad passed away, before I
met James.

I feel her energy fill my body and I'm open to this new day.

Though I can't express out loud the plans that are bubbling inside
me, I allow them to fill me up with new purpose.

*I will not be held captive by this empty life any longer.*

*I am already free and I feel so powerful.*

*No one can take my thoughts from me.*

*And there is SO much freedom in thought!*

*In clear thought.*

I make my way to the bathroom.

He's already in the kitchen having coffee with his mother.

I can hear their quiet, serious conversation down the hall.

I splash my face with cool water and take my time gathering myself
for whatever is to face me today.

*I can do this.*

I see myself in the mirror and notice a glimmer of sparkle in my
eyes.

*There you are.*

*You are going to be okay.*

*You are going to see your Babies very soon, very soon.*

My face is boney.

I'm too thin.

I weigh myself and am shocked that I'm only a hundred and five pounds, fifteen pounds short of my ideal weight.

*You are way too thin, Girl.*

*What have you done to yourself?*

I feel my fragile face and splash it again and again with cold water as more thoughts of my Mom come to mind.

*What would she be telling me right now?*

*I have to call her.*

Just the thought of her gives me more courage and determination to begin my journey back to myself, my Children, and my life.

Back to breathing effortlessly again, I walk into the kitchen.

He sees me and smiles. "We've been talking."

I fill my coffee cup and eye where the cell phone may be.

I can't see it.

*Of course, he's wearing it.*

"We found a place in Phoenix where I can get some help," he says.

"You know how my weight has been bothering me?" he continues, despite my lack of interest.

"It's from smoking and mixing alcohol with your medication,"
I blurt.

His face reddens.

I tried to help him lose the extra pounds with better meal plans, fewer sweets, less alcohol, and more exercise, but he found excuses and only blamed the meds for his weight gain.

I tried to tell him it was simply a side effect that would dissipate with time and to quit mixing his meds with alcohol, but he made more excuses and that was that.

The "poor-me" whining continued and the drinks kept being poured.

"You know why I drink!" he protests. "You don't get it. I can't help it."

He gets up out of his chair and slams his coffee cup beside me on the counter.

I ignore his aggression and turn my attention to his mother: "What is it that you found, Rose?"

Before his mother can reply he stomps away to put his shoes on.

She pats the table for me to sit down beside her.

I can tell she's distraught.

Her eyes are puffy and she holds her coffee cup with both of her frail, aging hands.

I have a sweep of compassion for her.

As a Mother, I too want to see no wrong in my children.

But I'd rather teach them through it then let them fall deeper into their bad behaviour.

*He is not my kid, so I am not taking it on anymore.*

*But there is no harm in hearing what she has to say in her attempts to help her son.*

We hear the slamming of the door as he leaves the house.

He's in one of his classic temper fits, and I'm grateful he's gone.

"Rose, I just need to call my Mom first."

Clearly anxious about giving me the phone, she nods her head.

Her eyes search for where she put it.

I reach out to touch her shoulder.

"I'll call her from right here," I say. "I just need to call my Mom."

Rose retrieves the phone from her desk that is nestled neatly in the corner of the dining room.

I thank her and call my Mother.

Her voice is comforting.

I haven't spoken to her in weeks.

I haven't seen her in over a year due to fear;

fear of him talking to Her,

fear of him doing something at home while I go see her,

fear of her intuition picking up that something isn't right

and then stressing her already worn heart into panic and worry.

*Mom!*

Her voice gives me hope.

I close my eyes and imagine I'm there with this woman who forgives over and over anyone who has ever hurt her.

This woman who has courage and fortitude.

This woman who would NOT want her daughter giving up on herself nor her happiness.

"So, I had a little chat with Andrew the other day. Both Children seem fine, but they need you, dear. Is your husband there for me to say a word or two?" She asks as we begin to wind down our conversation.

My heart squeezes so hard in my chest it hurts.

*Yay, my Son!*

*You called your Mummu as you promised.*

There's no risk in hinting to her that I'm not in a happy house, but I don't want Rose to know exactly what I'm saying.

I fear it getting back to him and beginning a series of offensive phone calls back to my Mother.

All I can reply with is the subtle truth: "Yes, Mom I'm so glad you had that chat! Yes they do! No, Mom, he's not here and he wouldn't want to talk."

She's silent for a moment.

She hears me.

It hurts me to know she feels any kind of slight or rejection.

I tear up.

"Well," She replies quietly, "tough beans on him then!"

*Oh, she is miffed!*

I smile through the brimming tears.

I chuckle and Rose looks quizzically at me.

"Yeah, Mom," I answer, "tough, bloody beans!"

We both laugh.

We laugh and laugh about this and that and I listen as she tells me about the adventures in the assisted-care facility where she resides.

*My Mother.*
*I love Her!*
We chat for a few more minutes until the phone beeps.
There's another call.
"Mom, I love you!" I don't want the call to end but I can't push
it. "Rose has another call coming through. No, she doesn't want
to talk either. Yup, tough beans on her too! I love you, Mom.
And Mom, call the kids. They would love to hear from their
Mummu again."
I make eye contact with Rose.
*Go ahead, tattle if you want.*
*Let him control you too.*
I answer the other line.
"You want to find me or should it be mom?"
It's my patient.
"I'm not sure if I should use a knife or just run my vehicle off the
road. Which would be less of a mess for my mom? I can't keep
letting her down."
I drop the phone.
I run for the door, grabbing Rose's car keys from the key holder we
made her one Mother's Day.
I drive as fast as I dare.

# CHAPTER 11

## Arizona

―〜―

*"So, like a poker player*
*after assessing an opponent,*
*I play my card."*
– Colleen Songs

Going to the rescue has now become second nature.

The thought of never severing our tie, never allowing me the
statement of independence that a divorce would bring me if I were
to end up his widow, pisses me right off.

I have thoughts of just letting him do it.

They scare me.

I know those thoughts are wrong.

I couldn't live with myself.

I value life too much.

*Or do I?*

*I did not protect the life I had with my own Children enough to get away from
him a long time ago.*

I beat myself up as I drive.

He's at the RV.

I feel it.

I pull into the park and see the truck.

*Well, he did not run off the road.*

I start trembling.

*What will I find?*

I take a deep breath and prepare myself for that one chance that he
might have really done himself in this time.

It's only been a few minutes from the time he left the house until
now, but it takes only a second to plunge a knife into your heart or
pull a trigger.

I tell myself a real attempt would not afford a phone call;
that this is just another control tactic.

*FRIG!*

*This is ridiculous!*

*It is like a bloody horror movie!*

I get out of the car and move towards the RV.

I open the door and step through.

And there he is,

in his chair,

freshly poured vodka in hand,

rocking incessantly,

agitated and red-faced.

"What the devil are you trying to pull now?" I shout. "Do you KNOW what you're putting your mother through? I KNOW you don't care about us anymore, but your own MOTHER?"

"I know what you're trying to do, Colleen. I know!" The pitch of his voice is higher than usual and full of venom.

"And what is that, James? Just what am I trying to do?" I know he's angry with my comment about mixing his meds and drinking in front of his mother.

I don't regret it.

*Maybe now she will see the other side of her son,*

*the one I have been married to.*

For him to be this angry he has obviously told her other reasons why his meds aren't working, why we weren't working.

If his mother knows the truth, it'll show him up.

"YOU!" he screams at me. "You made that comment about my meds and drinking in front of my mother!"

*Bingo.*

"Well stop doing it!" I hurl back at him. "It says not to for a reason!"

"You just don't get it. YOU JUST DON'T GET IT, COOOOOLLLLL EEEEEN!"

He stares at me, sips at his drink, and looks away.

Rocking.

Rocking.

I cringe when he says my name.

I have come to hate when he says it; polluting my person, my family chord.

I stay silent.

I wait to respond.

I breathe.

No words will get through to him right now.

I cannot afford to let my plan slip.

I must figure out his mind so that I know how to get us both through this, and then I must calm his mother who is probably out of her mind with worry.

*Jayne will call for me to come help her prepare for the baby.*

*And as soon as my tickets are booked I am free.*

"Give me your cell," I switch my voice to calm and soothing.

I reach my hand out to him.

He looks at me and I look at my patient.

I see a body with no conscience.

I see an empty shell.

It chills me.

I'm so tired of this.

*I do not want to feel.*

*I do not want to panic,*

*nor grieve,*

*nor cave,*

*nor crumble*

*anymore.*

*I will think only of my Children.*

*They need me.*

*I need them.*

*With him so close again, they are not safe.*

*Just focus on getting home.*

I kneel beside him, my outstretched hand still waiting to receive his cell phone. "I need to set your mother at ease. I left in such a rush. I need to tell her you're okay and that I'm with you. That is all."

He hands me his phone.

"Colleen, is he okay?" I hear her voice, broken and sniffing.

"Rose, we're at the RV. He's okay, just upset. Want to talk to him?"

I hand the phone to him.

He listens for a bit, offering soft 'Uh hums' in reply to the pleading words I can faintly hear.

Feeling a little warm and dizzy I sit on the sofa.

I lay my head in my hands and breathe.

*Jesus!*

*For crying out loud!*

*Give me strength until I hear from Jayne!*

He hands the phone back to me.

I take it without lifting my head.

"Yes, Rose? Are you ok?" I ask.

"Colleen, he's agreed to go to Arizona to get the help we've found. I told him about it last night. We didn't get the chance to tell you about it. Please take him there," her voice is pleading.

*So this is what he was concocting!*

"I would go, but I have to take care of my Aunt. I'm all she has." Rose's voice trails off into soft sobs.

She's sure she has found the answer.

My heart breaks for her as a mother.

I would not give up hope for my Children either, but I cannot give her any reassurances.

This is just another one of his ploys.

*He mentioned some plan last night and set me up so that I could not say no to her.*

Unbelievable.

So believable.

I shake my head with disbelief and urge my body to stand.

*God, you are really pissing me off.*

*Can I really give him any more of me?*

*Will I get out alive this time?*

The risks are higher and higher every day.

I battle with my conscience and my desire to leave right now.

Pacing back and forth, I search my mind for wisdom.

*This is no longer my burden.*

*Leave right now.*

*Just go!*

*Just Go!*

*JUST GO!*

*She can damn well take her own son to Arizona!*

*I can pack up my belongings, get my Jeep out of storage, and just go.*

*He does not WANT help!*

*He wants control.*

*He only wants to feed his excuses.*

*He has no intention of getting further help.*

*He is just stringing us along.*

*Arizona is only an excuse to keep me further away from my Children, to prove his point, and to gain his mother's support.*

I'm bitter and angry.

*WHY?*

My inner-self screams!

I look up at him.

He stares at me with that look in his eye that sends me over my temper limit:

smug,

steady,

knowing he's getting his own way.

He has me cornered and he knows it.

I live always at risk, knowing he WILL kill himself and that I couldn't live with myself if there was even a drop of hope to prevent it.

He'll never understand my reasons why, but he uses them to manipulate me anyway.

He views my reasons as a weakness that he exploits.

*If I drop him and go right now, he will call my Children and damage them with his revenge.*

*Worse, he'll go to them and…*

*I shake my head in an effort to avoid thinking about what he would do.*

*This is my cross to bear!*
I make my decision.
*Rose cannot take him.*
*She cannot leave her Aunt as there is no one else reliable to care for her.*
*They are so attached and Aunty is so fragile.*
*And I let him into our lives.*
*I kept him in our lives by trying too hard for way too long to make it work.*
I know what I have to do.
*I have to get HIM as far away from my Children as I can.*
*This will get him away from them.*
*He is too close to them here.*
*That is it!*
*THIS will work!*
*He doesn't have me cornered when really, this is helping me!*
*He will not be able to hurt them when I do NOT return from Jayne's.*
*He will be too far away to get home before I do!*
So, like a poker player after assessing an opponent, I play my card.
"Fine," I tell him, feigning resolution. "We'll leave in the morning on a few conditions."
I leave him hanging.
I need to buy some time to figure this out and rework my plan.
I find the keys I came with.
I walk out of the RV without saying another word and drive back to his mother's.
I need to console her and get some sleep before we head out in the morning,
to Arizona.
*Just a few more weeks…*

# CHAPTER 12

## First Sight Unseen

"I try to sort out when things started to turn.
It's a never-ending catalogue that I loop through in my mind,
looking for answers."
– Colleen Songs

Déjà vu.

I've been here before.

The destination isn't the same, but the feelings are.

I think about that as I rest my head in my hand while leaning on the passenger side window.

My patient and I have been on the road for hours since leaving Rose's house that morning.

We're going to Vancouver for a few days before heading to Arizona, term one of my conditions to accompany him.

He's cheery and apparently hopeful.

His body language is that of a child who just got his own way after whining until his mother gave in:

smiling,

smug,

tapping his fingers on the steering wheel as the radio plays some empty version of Tina Turner.

*"What's Love Got to Do With It," all right.*

*He does not even know what it means.*

I'm tired.

I'm struggling with my faith,

with my reserve,

with "Why?" this is happening.

I curse God:

once my friend,

now my foe.

I have a lump in my throat and as we drive it grows larger.

It becomes like a tumour:

a disease amassed from too many sips of remorse mixed with regret.

Swallowing is a grinding task.

*You'd better pull through on your end of the deal, Big Guy.*

*You'd better be sure my Children are safe.*

*You'd better make sure I get home alive to make this right for them and to ease their broken hearts.*

*Our lives matter as much as his does, you fucking asshole!*

I choke back my tears as a wave of bitter emotion splashes over me.

I was so close to being free of him and resent the sudden change of plans that I know are in vain.

Even though I convinced myself this worked on my behalf, I know what is to come and I feel the fatigue set deep inside my bones.

And I am pissed off.

Pissed off that I got suckered into an extension of this road trip from hell.

*There has to be a reason for this!*

*I miss my Children!*

I regret cussing out God, but he should know that I'm pissed off at him.

It's not like you can keep a secret from your own conscience.

*If You really are the ALL-KNOWING mighty Being that You profess to be, then You should know the all and everything behind why I'm so pissed off without me having to explain it!*

*Isn't that right, Mr. Universe?*

I focus on the passing trees out my window,

try to forget the aching pain,

and concentrate on my plan.

We drive through Alberta and into the mountains of British Columbia.

My beloved mountains!

Memories swarm over me of the many road trips the Children and I took together through these mountains to see all four of their Grandparents.

Summers of lake time and warm hugs.

*I am barely even alive without my kids!*

I send a subliminal plea to my Daughter and Son.

*My Babies,*

*please know I love you!*
*I am coming home soon, I promise.*
I visualize my thoughts reaching them in spirit just as the song
"You're Gonna Miss This" starts playing on the radio.
I try and block out the images that the song depicts.
Every lyric reminds me of what I have been missing.
Precious moments that I can never have back.
I'll only be able to ask my Children to fill in the blanks of these
days I am missing.
Treasured time passes so quickly.
Hard times pull and stretch 'til you want to scream "Is it over yet?"
*We have such a short yet precious time with our kids, and I'm missing it!*
*"Oh GOD, why is this happening?"*
Tears well up in my eyes and I let them fall.
I don't want to stop them.
They are the closest thing I have in this moment to my Children.
I'm caving inside out.
I let the song take me to the hollow grave of defeat where I'm
hopelessly being buried.
I succumb to the weight of this miserable trip.
Tears once again turn to sobs,
sobs to scattered breaths,
scattered breaths to pounding heart and exhausted body.
I feel his hand on my arm and it makes me recoil.
I push him away.
"We have some hope now," he says quietly. "You know, for me to
be well, for us to get back together, and to plan a life just for us."
I shake my head.
*"Shut up!"* I utter under my breath.
He tunes the radio to another station, a news channel, and leaves
me and my thoughts alone.
He is probably thinking how great he is since he is letting me see
my niece Mae during the stopover in Vancouver.

It is a joke.

He is only going to display his 'poor me, look what the kids have done to us' act on her, one of my closest family members.

The last time they met she told me she had noticed things weren't right.

She noticed the things that I was trying to deny.

But she didn't push and simply observed.

She is kind and doesn't meddle.

That's the kind of person she is.

This time I won't be in denial.

I need to see her, though I must protect her as well.

God knows my patient can turn on a dime.

I try and clear my head of 'supposes' and refocus on my plan.

*Faith the size of a mustard seed can move mountains.*

*Seeing Mae is my mustard seed.*

The monotony of the drive takes me into my memories from that day at the doctor's office until now.

Coming on nine years.

I try to sort out when things started to turn.

It's a never-ending catalogue that I loop through in my mind, looking for answers.

I hear a voice in my head:

it's strong,

it's clear,

it belongs to the One with the footprints.

'Footprints in the Sand' has always been one of my favourite poems.

I revere it so much that I can't put it to music like I've done with many other poems I've either written or connected to.

The image of Mary Stevenson's poem is vivid in my mind as I hear the voice recite it through my thoughts:

One night I dreamed
I was walking along the beach with the Lord.
Many scenes from my life flashed across the sky.
In each scene I noticed footprints in the sand.
Sometimes there were two sets of footprints,
other times there was one set of footprints.

This bothered me because I noticed
that during the low periods of my life,
when I was suffering from
anguish, sorrow or defeat,
I could see only one set of footprints.

So I said to the Lord,
"You promised me Lord,
that if I followed you,
you would walk with me always.
But I have noticed that during
the most trying periods of my life
there have only been one
set of footprints in the sand.
Why, when I needed you most,
were you not there for me?"

The Lord replied,
"The times when you have
seen only one set of footprints,
are when I carried you."

I open my heart to the conscious thought of my Higher Being and
plead for it to speak to me.
*Guide me please!*
*I'm sorry for cursing You!*
*You know why.*

*You even know what I am missing that has brought me to this very moment of
hating him and being angry with You.*

*Help me see that I can still trust in ANY kind of a higher purpose to
this mess!*

"You can waste this time too and keep searching for things you
have no control over," says the Voice.

The Voice of 'real-eyes-ation' flips a light upon my
muddled reflections.

"Or you can stop wallowing and be ready for Life when your time
comes. Stop crying and get working on YOU!"

It severs my search for understanding

And,

like a heavy cloak unzipped,

doubt and anger fall away.

*I do not need to understand my patient anymore!*

*I need to know Me once again!*

*I need to ready MYSELF for my return!*

*I AM going to make it home!*

Without hesitation I blow my nose, wipe my eyes, and take a sip of
the water I have tucked beside me.

A wind rushes into my lungs, releasing sour, damp breath and
replacing it with fresh oxygen.

My blood picks up speed inside my veins.

A sudden urge to drive hits me.

*I wish he wasn't such a control freak and would let me drive more often.*

Fortunately, upon each departure, he happened to be sober.

I acknowledge the divine intervention in that bit of serendipity.

*I guess the Good Lord DOESN'T give us more than we can handle!*

*That said, James doesn't hand over the keys any easier than he does his phone.*

*He needs full control.*

I neither ask nor argue much about this.

I'm not crazy about driving a one-tonne truck hauling a twenty-
nine-foot Fifth Wheel.

But right now I want to drive!
I imagine I'm at the wheel and in control of this newest leg of
MY journey.
I am the driver!
I meditate on the feeling of freedom that the image provides me.
*I am starting over with the things I CAN change today!*
*I am peaceful and this state lets me calmly and methodically go back in time so*
*that I can cleanse my memories and my Self.*
I drive through time as I would through an old neighbourhood I
once resided.


Everything was good in the beginning,
just like it's supposed to be.
After seeing Blue Eyes in the doctor's office for the first time, it
took me a few months to get the courage to walk into his place
of business.
I had told him I was a singer and he said he wanted a copy of
my CD.
A few months later, when the first professional demo of my very
own songs lay tangible in my hands, it gave me a good excuse to
find him.
On a day when I had several errands to run in town, I drove my
Children to school instead of making them take the dreaded hour-
long bus ride.
I was having a "good hair day" and felt skinny so I got up the
nerve to walk into his thriving business with my CD in hand.
A lady in her fifties was behind the till at the gas station/carwash
that he claimed was his.
She was warm and cheery, but I instantly got nervous because I
realized I didn't know his name.
I asked her quickly if she could give the CD to the owner for me.
"You mean James?" she asked, and smiled.
I blushed and said "Yes," hoping we meant the same person.

By the time I got home, I had an e-mail from James thanking me
for the CD.

I also had an invite for tea the next time I was in town which
confirmed that James was indeed Blue Eyes.

My heart skips a little when I recall that encounter.

Skips and saddens.

I swallow and allow the feeling to come and go.

We started our relationship slowly, getting to know one another as
friends over the next few months.

I didn't want to rush into anything and my Children were sensitive.

They were still adjusting to the changing world of our separated
family, even though Wayne and I had made sincere attempts to
keep things light for them.

I had moved into a small house on the west side of town and had
helped Wayne move and set up his house at the east side.

We both lived at equal distances from the Children's school.

It was hard on Wayne.

He still loved me.

I needed to leave.

We had married too young.

We were both changing in good ways, but we were growing
farther apart.

I loved him dearly but I wasn't in love with him.

I hadn't known the difference until then and had to carry the
gargantuan load of explaining my wavering feelings to him.

"I'm not in love with you" are the hardest words to say to someone
you love.

In time, the transition from husband and wife to separate lives
became smooth.

We were in a routine.

On Wayne's days off he'd have the Children and that was when I'd
see James.

I didn't want the Children to be introduced to another man until he was tested and true.

As a friend, James introduced me to the New Age spiritualism that gave me the "AHA!" feeling in my heart standard religion had never done.

We talked and debated over spiritual thought and ideas for hours on the phone after the Children were asleep.

Our long night-time chats continued into the days and we started seeing each other more frequently.

I was happy about getting to know James and experiencing this newfound freedom and love.

Everything and everyone seemed happy.

*Where did you go, James?*
As my patient grips the wheel, staring out over the road, I look at him.

The man sitting in the driver's seat is not the man I fell in love with.

I turn away and focus on my mission of emotional cleansing.

I let the whir of the passing trees pull me back in time.

On the summer before meeting James, my Dad had passed away.

Mom was still living in their apartment.

Every day her calls to me sounded lonelier and lonelier.

Her voice was getting thinner and thinner.

I was afraid she would soon be a living ghost, and so I decided to move her into my house with me.

I had the space.

The main living room was basically my bedroom anyway.

I slept there in order to be close to the Children at night.

That meant there was an extra bedroom for my Mother.

She moved in with the help of my Sisters and we made her cozy and comfy in her new home.

She was no extra work.

The Children loved their Mummu and she was my rock.

I look back now and wish I had kept her home with me.

I wish a thousand times plus infinity that I had not even considered dating for at least another decade.

I thought I could do it all.

I thought I could take on my own household, work days (and the occasional evenings) while Mom watched the Children, and quietly see someone who touched my spiritual side.

One afternoon when two of my Sisters were visiting with Mom and I, he came over.

I was happily surprised to see him, introduced him as my friend, and invited him to join us.

When we were all seated on the porch having tea and a chat, he put his bare feet on my lap in front of my family.

It wasn't the act of politely resting his feet on my lap,

it was the way he did it.

He sat across from me,

leaned into the back of his chair,

and placed both of his feet on my lap.

Not gently.

It was a thud.

It was like a hammer pounding a stake into the ground.

It hurt a little.

I actually jumped as his feet hit my lap and he sat back in his chair with smug possessiveness.

My face turned all sorts of red

from scarlet,

to beet,

to shame.

Such impropriety in front of my Mother!

Such a statement that should have warned me to think twice before dating this guy further!

My Mother laughed it off to ease my embarrassment and teased him with, "Well, someone's making himself comfortable around here. Maybe we can get the roof looked at, eh, Colleen?"

The glances from my Sisters were of complete disapproval.

Their stern faces from the past trigger another 'real-eyes-ation' in me today.

That was it.

*That was when it all started.*

I'm shocked out of my memory trance.

*Oh my God-ness!*

*It started that early?*

*His dominance started that early!*

*I allowed it THAT early?*

My introspective search for clarity provides fodder for my inner bully.

*Stupid!*

*Stupid!*

*Stupid, naïve girl!*

I begin to grieve the time I have lost;

all the little painful things that could have possibly been prevented all these years

from that painful thud on my lap

to the excruciating tears my Children and I have shed.

They wouldn't have happened had I pushed his feet off my lap and asked him to leave.

# CHAPTER 13

## A Kiss…

"Thought is the smallest particle of creation.
When it becomes dis-eased
it becomes a warped sense of reality
where the dwellers who love you reside."
– Colleen Songs

We descend into the Okanagan Valley to pick up my Mom.
We moved her there a few years after she moved in with me.
With her health becoming more delicate and her wanting to be
closer to her favourite church, it was a hard decision for us to make
but the best one for her.
I feel fortunate to have had a bit of time with her in my home,
living amongst some of her family that she so missed.
My patient and I had made arrangements to pick her up and
take her with us to Merritt to visit with my sister Ellen on our
way through to Vancouver where we would visit Mae then cross
the border.
This is term two of our agreement.
It's all I can do to not spill my heartbreak onto my Mom.
She's so fragile now.
She is delighted when we arrive at her little apartment.
She hugs us both warmly and points in the direction of her little,
blue twill overnight bag sitting by the door.
James picks it up and we follow her out to the truck.
She is thrilled to be going on an adventure.
My heart tugs and I smile as I watch her fragile frame come to life.
She has forgotten about our phone call and the rejection of not
being able to talk to James about her concerns after having that
chat with Andrew.
She is the most forgiving person I know.
She tells everyone in the home that she's going away for a few days
with her Daughter and Son-in-Law.
He is patient with her.
She's excited to have one more ride out in the country, especially
pulling a trailer.
It feels like old times and brings me back to fond memories of the
times we shared when Dad was still alive.
She misses him a lot.
It's in her every conversation:

Your Dad this,

Your Dad that.

My patient doesn't want to be seen as anything but perfect.

We've already settled the "I'm only doing this because I want you to hear from your own family what your kids have done to us!" argument last night as we said our 'goodnights' to each other from our separate beds.

I soothed him with passive lies.

"Let's just have a good visit with Mom," I said, "so she doesn't see that we're over. It would stress her out. I want this little trip to be pleasant for her."

Mom asks if she can stay in the RV with us once we got parked in Merritt, but she can barely make it up the stairs.

I appease her by explaining that Ellen has a room all ready for her and is anxious to have us over.

I get a glimpse of the old James for a few moments.

He's charming and thoughtful.

He asks her questions about her new friends.

"Everyone is so old there," she huffs.

He laughs and they chat away.

I try not to break down.

Why isn't he like this all the time?

Nonetheless, after only a couple of hours into our visit with my Sister, he wants to go.

I can read his body language:

fingers tapping,

feet twitching,

he's ready for a drink.

I tell him I'd like to stay longer and visit with my family before heading out the next morning.

He asks me to take him back to the RV and then I can come back to enjoy the rest of the evening, returning whenever I want.

We get in the truck and head back to the RV.

"Don't even think about calling the kids, Colleen," he says, lecturing me as soon as he starts the engine. "You'll ruin everything and they don't care anyway. They don't give a shit about me, nor do they care about what they're making you go through."

His face is redder with every vowel he utters.

"I just want to see my Mother," I respond. "Is that okay with you? I have one day."

I panic, thinking he'll change his mind about me returning to Ellen's.

I imagine what I will do to him once he falls asleep if he prevents me from having more time with my Mom.

*Do not think those things, or you will never see your kids again for sure and he'll win.*

He parks in front of the RV and reaches under his seat for a pack of cigarettes.

I breathe, trying not to show how anxious I am to leave him and go back.

I need my family's love, humour, strength, and resilience to get me through this.

"Just relax and enjoy your evening," I say to him. "You've driven for two days. Just get rest, okay?" I try and appease him.

He softens a little. "I'm just so scared for you. You're too kind and it hurts me that the kids have hurt you so much and…"

"I've got it!" I interrupt.

*I can't listen to your sick brain any longer.*

It feels like his hands are tightening around my throat as he stalls me with these tiring warnings.

"I'll be fine," I say. "I'll play Scrabble with Mom. I can't say or do anything to get her stressed so I won't be telling her or Ellen anything. Mom's too fragile. I'm just going to have time with her just like I let you have time with your Mom. Thank you for being okay to pick her up and bring her along with us."

I purposefully try and make him feel like the hero of the day so I can get the hell away from him.

I slide over to the driver's seat and fake a smile.

He slowly hands over the keys.

He is too close to me.

"You must be tired," I say. "Go eat and rest."

I attempt to push him out the door so I can drive away.

He leans into the truck and kisses me.

I'm surprised by this gesture.

He has not kissed me in...??

I have forgotten how long:

maybe a year,

maybe more.

I'm sickened at the touch of his lips,

a stranger's lips.

I feel nauseous.

I scramble to leave, pushing him clear of the truck door.

I start the engine.

I want to scrub my face and clean my mouth from his kiss.

I drive away.

I wait until I'm around the corner to burst into tears.

I wipe my mouth with the back of my hand until my lips are swollen.

I curse his mother for making me go on this trip.

I was so close to being free of him!

*"WHY?" I scream at the windshield as I drive back to my sister's. "GOD, I just want to GO!!!"*

*"Why am I being held here?" I hit the steering wheel.*

*"If I leave now, he'll call the kids!" I reason.*

*"He'll call and scar them deeper!" I fear.*

*"I'm trapped!" I submit.*

*"All I did was love him!" I implore.*

*"All my Children and I did was love him and build a home together!"*
*I anguish.*
*"Why are we being so deeply punished just for being a family?" I beg.*
*"I've stood by him!" I negotiate.*
*"We've moved wherever he needed to be well!" I admit.*
*"My Children always made the best of things and were respectful!" I enforce.*
*"They're INNOCENT!" I demand.*
*"They're only Children and I let them down!" I concede.*
*"Is that why I'm being punished?" I postulate.*
*"I sent them to their Father's to be safe from this tyrant and I'M being*
*punished?" I challenge.*
*"GOD, Why have YOU forsaken ME?" I cry until my voice is hoarse.*
*"It's a TWO-WAY STREET!" I amen.*
I do not recall making it to my Sister's place.
I do not recall talking or laughing with her and our Mom
over Scrabble.
There are pictures to prove I was there but I recall nothing.
I do not recall getting back to the RV.
I'm a victim of his thoughts.
*He thought he could just kiss me and make things better,*
*use the one thing he has starved me of to control me,*
*and strip me of my mind along with his.*
Thought is the smallest particle of creation.
When it becomes dis-eased
it becomes a warped sense of reality
where the dwellers who love you
reside.

# CHAPTER 14

## Puppy Love

*"Guilt cannot look kindness in the eye without shrivelling,
so it stays away."*
– Colleen Songs

I go alone to my Sister's early the next morning for a coffee and to say goodbye.

My patient doesn't come with me.

He voices that he doesn't want to face the family, my family, this morning.

*They see through him and he knows it.*

Guilt cannot look kindness in the eye without shrivelling, so it stays away.

I say goodbye to my Mother.

I let her gentle hugs console me inside the places I can't reveal to her.

*God knows where her love needs to go.*

She smells of baby shampoo and talcum powder.

Her fragile, pink skin is soft as I kiss her cheek.

I love this woman,

this woman who made me strong,

this woman who went through so much for her family,

who gave up so much for her greatest love of all:

her husband and children.

I hold her and silently send her my love.

*I owe it to you to be strong now, Mom,*

*to pay homage to the sacrifices you have made for me.*

*I am sorry for the things I allowed him to say to you and the time I wasted on a man who did not really love us.*

*I'm sorry I didn't just keep you home with me and not bother with him.*

I am aching.

I tear myself away from my loving family and drive back to the RV where I see he has everything ready for our trip to the coast.

Next stop, Vancouver.

Swallowing tears, I back the truck up to the hitch, step out, and allow him to take over.

As I walk around doing the final camp cleanup my longing turns to Mae, my niece, only two years younger and my best friend.

Mae is the one person who knows me better than anyone else,
even myself.

I'm always drawn to her when I need the bare truth.

*She has words for me now, blunt and honest words I need to hear.*

*Those words will help drive me forward.*

I know my family doesn't understand me for the decisions I've
made that have put me in this mess.

But if I were to tell them the truth,

they would come running to get me.

This would put them in harm's way and heighten his fury.

He would only rage at them,

blame them,

criticize them.

He would blame my Children for ruining us.

*I cannot risk it,*

*I could not bear it,*

*I have my plan and I must stick to it.*

*The truth will come out when it is safe to do so,*

*when I am safe and strong enough to set it free.*

We head out of Merritt and begin the journey to Vancouver.


It's a warm and sunny day.

I take in the rolling, arid hills of the countryside.

This is one of the areas of British Columbia that my Dad fell in
love with.

"This is real cattle and cowboy country," he'd say.

With so many years working the mines and highways of British
Columbia and Yukon, he knew many of the original farming and
ranch families in the region.

I allow myself to forget whom I'm driving with and begin to
imagine riding with Dad in his old '57 Buick.

I imagine his voice telling me of this lake and that fishing trip or the time he went hunting with this friend or that son-in-law in the Chilcotin.

*Dad, I am sorry.*
*I did not listen to your whispers.*
*You never knew James, but you knew him from Heaven.*
*You whispered so many warnings.*
*You waved those little red flags.*
*Oh, Dad!*
*Do not stop whispering now!*
*I am finally listening!*

My patient and I are approaching the Fraser Valley when he takes an unexpected exit.

I look at him in wonder.

"Uh, aren't we supposed to take the Langley exit?" I ask him.

Nervous twinges start to rise in my gut.

He smiles and looks at me. "I have a surprise for you."

I am nauseous and unsure.

Surprises have only meant something bad of late.

My imagination goes wild.

I have thoughts of being locked up in an unknown house and never allowed out, thoughts of being the victim of a murder/suicide.

I feel panic sweep its grip around my throat like a vice.

It calms down when we pull up to a seniors' complex.

*Whew, not a place he would exactly dump and bury me.*

I allow myself to relax a bit.

I let out a nervous giggle.

*What is he up to?*

My patient comes around to my side of the truck and opens the door for me, a gesture he hasn't offered me in years.

Out of guarded curiosity, I allow him to lead me out of the vehicle and around the white flower-dotted complex to a door where he rings the bell.

A lady in her late seventies answers.

She is accompanied by a decked-out walker.

It has reflectors, bright orange flags, and a flowered basket with pockets for her purse, umbrella, and hat.

I have to smile because Mom always joked around about having a walker with a Harley-Davidson license plate on it.

She thinks bikers and motorcycles are so cool.

"You must be James!" the elderly woman says, welcoming us warmly.

She shakes James' hand and offers her hand to me.

I shake her hand gently.

She looks so dainty but actually has a strong boney grasp that I didn't expect.

I smile at her while wondering why we stopped here, and then I notice a small dog leash with a spool of "goody" bags attached to her walker handle.

"Well, come on in and I'll show you the pup." She whirls around in her walker so quickly that I jump to assist her, thinking she might topple over.

*Did she just say pup?*

*Please do not tell me we are getting a dog!*

We follow her down a hallway that smells of peppermints and Depends, powder and yes, puppies.

Two little black and brown Yorkshire terriers leap up behind the baby gate that blocks the doorway of their assigned room.

Despite their cuteness, I instantly get a knot in my stomach.

One little guy is bigger than the other and he catches my eye.

I don't go towards him.

I'm hesitant.

*What is the deal here?*

"You say they're purebred Yorkies?" my patient asks.

"Oh yes," she replies, reaching over the gate to pat the big guy on the head. "But this guy is too big for me to pick up. He's from my daughter's litter. He's the one I'm selling. He might be the milkman's pup, so to speak."

She chuckles and stands up, holding onto her walker.

My patient reaches in to give the pup a pat on the head.

"So what do you think?" he asks me with a smile. "Would this fill the hole in your heart and get you to relax?"

I choke back my anger.

*NOTHING CAN REPLACE MY CHILDREN!*

*YOU WANT TO REPLACE MY CHILDREN WITH A DOG?*

*OH MY GOD!*

Tears well up and I try to disguise my anger in front of this innocent woman.

I excuse myself and walk back to the truck.

I close my eyes and swallow lumps of hatred and mixed emotions.


I remember Sandy, my little apricot-coloured mini poodle that I had before my patient came into our lives.

Sandy was Sissy's birthday present when she turned three.

Sissy has been an animal lover from the first time she could hold her own teddy bear.

She would sleep with all of her bears tucked in and around her little body.

I remember Wyatt, the bulldog my patient bought himself for his fortieth birthday.

Wyatt was too big and playful for Sandy, so my patient gave Sandy, OUR dog, to HIS mother.

He said it was safer that way.

Wyatt wouldn't mean to hurt Sandy, but he just might injure her.

My patient certainly hurt my kids.

They were distraught.

"It is a greater act of love to think of Sandy first," he told them.

*Funny, he never thought of anyone else but himself first.*

I remember Jesse, the bulldog my patient bought as a companion for Wyatt.

Jesse was affectionate and needy.

My patient didn't like him as much because Jesse asked for love.

He said it was too difficult to manage both dogs, so he gave Jesse away too.

*The kids and I did everything anyway.*

*He barely did a damn thing.*

Sandy eventually got old and upon her last few hours of life we argued about letting the kids say goodbye.

He said it would be awful for the kids to see their dog sick.

She died in the arms of my mother-in-law instead of the arms of my Children where she belonged.

But it was us, along with the Children, who took her lifeless body to the vet clinic for disposal.

It would be too hard on his mother, he said.

I remember fighting with my patient at the vet clinic about whether to just let them dispose of her or get her cremated.

He said he wasn't going to spend that kind of money on a dead dog.

I wanted to honour her little life by giving her a proper burial.

I lost the argument and led two sad and solemn Children out to the vehicle.

But before we pulled away, I told him to stop.

I ran back into the vet clinic and asked that Sandy be cremated instead of thrown in the garbage dump.

I knew my patient would be angry at how much it would cost to cremate a dead dog, so I made sure to order the most expensive options:

a tiny silver urn,

a carved oak box,

and an engraved brass plate.

We grieved so hard, the Children and I.

Deeper than anyone knew,

alone,

just the three of us.

Then Wyatt got sick.

Just before we sent Sissy to her dad's, my patient became more and more toxic.

He wouldn't take care of his dog any longer.

I could see Wyatt's health and happiness declining.

He lost patches of hair, and we couldn't control his digestion.

He was one of those animals who feel your every mood.

He grieved when we did.

He comforted us at the first sign of tears.

I couldn't keep up with Wyatt's care on top of everyone else's, so my patient gave him away instead of simply loving him.

*He would rather sit and rock in his stupid chair drinking and cursing us than walk and brush his faithful sweet Bully.*

A young couple from Regina adopted him.

They knew all about bulldogs and promised to provide him with the ultimate bulldog life.

But I'll never forget Wyatt's eyes looking out the window of the front door when we left him behind, so hurt and rejected.

I sent him silent thoughts of love.

He was much better in his new loving adoring home than in our crumbling, empty cave of despair.

The Children learned, one more time, the greater act of love.

This time it was justifiable,

for Wyatt's sake.


I hear his footsteps.

He opens the door on the driver's side and passes me the pup.

"I don't want a puppy," I say quietly.

He continues to place a bag of dog food and a leash into the back seat.

He's smiling and it annoys me.

*Smug asshole.*

I feel my face flushing and I push the puppy away onto the driver's seat.

"I don't WANT a puppy!" I throw the words at him with mounting anger.

"It will do you good," he says as he gets into his seat and puts the puppy on the console.

He starts the engine and we pull away.

"You don't care what's good for me!" I spew. "You never did and you never will. Everything is all about you. From the beginning! Everything has been about YOU! You don't care what I need, or want, or feel, or do! NOTHING is ever good enough. You used me and my Children like we were some label on a life you claim you had but you NEVER cared!"

The puppy licks my arm and I pull away.

*Sweetie, you do not stand a chance in this world with him.*

My patient remains silent.

"Now you listen to me!" I continue on my rampage. It feels so good to yell at him. "This puppy is YOUR idea. You never even asked me. You're only doing this to keep me because you know I could never leave a puppy behind. YOU are responsible for this animal. I am NOT! Do you hear me?"

As my voice rises, the puppy sinks lower on the console and whines.

"FINE!" exclaims my patient. "I'm just trying to help you get over those damn kids!"

I start laughing in disgust at his idiotic thoughts. "GET OVER MY CHILDREN!!! You ARE insane!!! My Children are not animals! THEY are NOT replaceable! YOU CANNOT EVEN COMPARE THE TWO!"

I'm beyond any further arguments.
My words fall on deaf ears and a vacant heart.
"Oh really?" he retorts with a chuckle. "You gave them up
so easily."

# CHAPTER 15

## Mae

———

*"I am responsible for having him in their lives.*
*I will carry that burden and protect them to the moon and back."*
— Colleen Songs

Before leaving his mother's place in Medicine Hat my patient
purchased an RV membership with Thousand Trails, a chain of
resorts and campgrounds.

There are only a couple of locations in Canada, one of which is
close to Mae at Cultus Lake – just an hour east of Vancouver.

My patient and I set up camp before heading out to see my niece.

My patient makes sure the puppy is confined and has food and
water, though he isn't smiling now that he knows I'm not lifting a
finger to help.

I'm even more anxious to get to Mae's.

*So close, yet so far.*

My patient lets her know we're settled and getting ready to
come over.

She then gives him the news that her parents, my Sister Lyn and
Brother-In-Law Terry, are there.

They're splitting up.

The news hits me like a hammer, taking the joy out of the forth-
coming visit.

I knew my Sister and her Husband had been having problems
and that this day was coming, but the reality of it now, along with
everything else, catches me off guard.

I know the weight of my situation sits heavily on Mae's heart, and
with the news of her own parents splitting after thirty-five years of
marriage, I want to be there for her now more than ever.

I stuff my own heartaches under my shirtsleeves and put on my
best smile for my niece and dearest friend.

My patient is good at faking things.

He had me fooled for years that he loved us.

I ask him to don his "good husband" mask and accompany me to
Mae's for dinner.

He's quiet but agrees to try and behave as normally as he can.

I feel like a lost child myself after hearing that one more set of my
family pillars is crumbling.

Five out of eleven isn't bad, considering the odds, and I am more than proud of the grace my sisters have displayed over the years. They, like I have been discovering about myself, gave their all and then some.

It's the 'then some' I need to work on,

protect,

hold back.

I begin questioning relationships, marriage, and commitment.

*I am so NEVER getting married again!*

We lock up the RV, satisfied that the puppy is content, and head out to Langley.

"There better be nothing said about the children to Mae," my patient says, breaking the beautiful silence as we drive. "I know she just doesn't understand what they've done to you, to us, so she'll take their side. Your family doesn't really care about me anyway. With her parents there, we should just be there for them. I don't even want to hear the children's names spoken out loud. Do you know what that does to me, Colleen?"

His words grate on my skin like nails on a chalkboard.

I fight back words that will only cause him to lose his temper before we arrive at our host's home.

I imagine whacking him on the head with a brick in my purse, but then I choose integrity and check my thoughts.

*Although they say it's the thought that counts…*

"You're only right about us being there for THEM right now," I keep my voice steady instead of sarcastic by imagining actually whacking him with that brick laden purse. "This is weird timing to have all of us over at once. They weren't expecting us and have some personal matters they're dealing with so we WILL make the best of it and be there for THEM."

*Whack.*

*Whack.*

I am not exactly reassuring him, but I confirm that I won't be talking about our situation.

When we arrive at Mae's her two young boys greet us with shrieks of laughter and squishes that make me feel like I'm being held by God Himself.

I'm strengthened by their hugs and my protective nature is empowered.

They call me Aunty Coco, my nickname passed on through a great niece who couldn't say my name.

It stuck.

I adore it when I am called Aunty Coco.

*I will do anything to protect my Children and ALL children from the poison of this man.*

*I am responsible for having him in their lives.*

*I will carry that burden and protect them to the moon and back.*

*Nothing will ruin this visit.*

*I am here for them.*

*I will not bring sadness and fighting into this beautiful home.*

My family's eloquence keeps their radar up and their tact in check but it takes only moments for them to detect that my energy is off.

I feel Terry's protectiveness over me and he graciously leads James to the patio to chat and get caught up.

I'm grateful for my Brother-In-Law.

Lyn is resting, so I remain in the kitchen, close to Mae.

She hugs me warmly when the boys give her a window between their fervent greetings.

"Are you all right?" she whispers in my ear.

A lump forms in my throat.

"Not really, but..." I whisper the only words I can muster.

*I am safe here.*

*If I just say, 'No, I have to leave him,' then I would have my family to protect me.*

*But what would the boys see?*

*What would James say out loud for them to hear?*
*The boys would be traumatized and they have enough heartache and confusion*
*to deal with right now.*
*What would he do as soon as he left the house?*
*He would call my Children.*
*I CANNOT tell anyone.*
*Not yet.*
*This is my cross to bear.*
"I'm okay, Mae," I lie. "The rest of this trip will be good for us."
I stop talking but I can't let her go.
We remain hugging.
I know she feels things aren't right.
I know she thinks I am wrong.
I can feel it.
*Of course she thinks that!*
*She only knows I abandoned my Children when they needed me most.*
*It does not matter how or why I went against every family code I was*
*raised with.*
*I cannot tell anyone that I HAD to, for my family's own safety.*
*Not yet.*
*I did it the wrong way, but I had to do it; and it all seemed to slip between my*
*fingers, right before my eyes.*
I feel James' glare on me and my neck begins to prickle.
Sure enough, he's turned to face us from the patio, his expres-
sion none-too-pleased.
*I've become fluent in reading his body language.*
Terry must feel the shift in James' energy too, but he keeps him
talking, like he's deliberately trying to give Mae and me time
to talk.
*He knows!*
Grateful for the boys running around, I release my hold on Mae
and turn my attention to them.
I purposefully make a point of playing cars with them for a while.

*Aunty Coco will not let anything disrupt your peace, my darling boys.*
*I will not bring his poison into your sanctuary.*
I glance over at Mae while I play with the kids.
My friend's shoulders are stooped as she prepares dinner.
*So many sorrows are giving her a heavy heart.*
*I am adding to her burden by being here.*
Whispering to the boys that I'm going to help their Mom for a bit,
I leave them alone to play and go to the aide of my best friend.
Her tears fall softly.
"I can't believe they're separating," she opens up without my
asking. "It's just so weird. I'm an adult and I understand why this is
happening, but it's still so hard. I feel like the ground is crumbling
beneath my feet. Everything you're going through and what your
kids are going through right now, it's just…" she can't finish.
She doesn't have to.
I hold her.
I'm not sure how to talk about her parents, my eldest Sister and
my Brother-In-Law.
Terry has always been in my life and I feel the effects of the loss
and fear that I may never be as close to him as I am now, that I'll
lose him over the passing years.
I've never known a time in my life when he wasn't a part of it.
However, Lyn comes first.
*Family first.*
*My Children first.*
*I know I cannot tell her my plan,*
*but I can hint.*
"I'll be going to see my girlfriend Jayne soon," I say quietly to
break the silence. I take a paring knife from a drawer and start
cutting vegetables with Mae. "She's expecting her first baby and
she's all alone."
Mae's stirring vegetables in the pan and the savoury promise of her
pasta sauce fills my nostrils.

I breathe in their sustenance.

I breathe in the life they promise around a dinner table with my family.

*Oh, please catch on to this plan of mine.*

*Please catch my secret.*

"I just can't imagine having a baby all alone," I continue, as though we're talking about recipes. "As soon as Jayne gives me the word that she's close to labour, James said he'll send me to her. I'll stay with her for a while."

Mae stops stirring and looks over to me.

"Okay," she whispers. "Promise you'll stay a good long while?"

I smile in answer and continue helping her prepare our meal.

We're interrupted by James and Terry coming inside from the patio.

My Sister comes up from the basement, composed from a nap and some time alone.

I greet her with hugs and we busy ourselves by setting the table.

During dinner I sit between the boys.

I've missed them so much.

I glance around at Lyn and look towards my Brother-In-Law, who is keeping conversation with James light and asking about our travel plans.

They gracefully ignore random comments James makes about their 'situation'. I admire my Sister and her Husband for their openness and desire to help the other move forward.

There's no hostility in their movements or angry looks towards each other tonight.

But James takes no notice.

His remarks and aloof attitude during dinner speaks louder than words.

I look at James and silently make a wish:

*I wish for a beautiful goodbye,*

*I wish for his peace of mind,*

*I wish for one last glimpse of the man I fell in love with long ago so that I may let HIM go.*
*He's the one I loved,*
*not this man.*
Tears well in my eyes and are about to fall.
I excuse myself from the table and go to the bathroom where I pretend to pee.
I wash my hands vigorously.
Towelling them off, I see they're shaking.
*Oh God, give me strength tonight!*
*Strength for Mae and strength for Lyn and Terry.*
I return to the table to find it already cleared.
My Brother-In-Law takes me by the arm and leads me to the garage.
I look over my shoulder to see where James is and notice that he's out on the patio, his back toward me, having a cigarette.
Lyn is walking toward him.
"How are you doing?" Terry asks me.
"Not good," I whisper.
My throat tightens and tears start to fall.
He hugs me and I cry into his chest.
*My other Dad.*
For the past couple of years, Terry and Lyn have been living on the coast running a bed and breakfast and learning many different alternative healing techniques.
The one method they've really connected to is called Emotional Freedom Technique, or EFT.
By placing one hand on certain points of the body, you use the other hand to gently tap. This tapping triggers your body to re-member and re-align your energy fields as you repeat positive mantras to yourself.
I had practiced EFT previously with a dear friend who had passed away.

I knew the benefits were remarkable, leaving me feeling fresh and my outlook on life or a certain situation crisper.

I miss that feeling.

Terry asks if I would like a session right now to carry me through this next phase of travel.

I nod my head.

He gives me a tissue to blow my nose and another hug.

"Lyn and I have been helping one another get through these changes with EFT, Colleen. It's a gift. Let's use it and do it quickly before James starts to wonder where you are."

My Brother-In-Law's voice soothes my soul and I feel the energy of the Universe already circling me,

grounding me,

strengthening me.

"We'll be brief, okay?" says Terry. "Lyn promised to keep James busy while we're out here."

With that reassurance, I let go of any anxiety.

"What do you need most right now, Colleen?" Terry asks quietly as he instructs me on where to begin tapping. "By some of the things he's telling us out on the deck I can detect some trouble between you two."

My heart sinks further into the pit of my stomach.

"What things?" I ask, clutching my stomach.

"Things that don't make sense," Terry chuckles. "Don't worry about it, just tell me what you need."

"I need to leave James," the words spill out of my mouth with quiet surrender.

*There!*

*I said it out loud!*

Weight leaves my body and I allow my mind to sink into the lightness, and reality, of my confession.

I begin tapping the tender spot on my collarbone and repeating after him:

"I'm no longer afraid to leave James and I totally and completely love and accept myself."

I repeat the phrase three times as I rub my collarbone.

Terry remains silent as I state my own mantras.

Unafraid.

"Even though I must leave James, I've done everything in my power to be the best wife to him that I could be and I totally and completely Love and accept myself."

I tap my forehead, then my temple.

I follow the process, repeating phrase after phrase of affirmations, tapping them into my body's memory.

With each phrase I feel stronger.

My body expands and cools.

My brain relaxes and softens within the cavity of my skull.

Even my hair seems to release its roots so as to fall more gracefully from my head.

I know my Brother-In-Law understands without my telling him.

Terry and Lyn have witnessed my turmoil and they're now at the ready to help me when I call for it.

They went for so long trying to keep things together for their own reasons.

*We all have reasons.*

*They know it was not me who left my Children.*

*They know it must be something beyond me to have made me do what I did and they didn't need to know why.*

*They know me.*

*I am not a bad mother.*

*I had to protect my Children at all costs.*

We hear a tap on the door.

It's the cue to stop.

Terry smiles at me and I feel his love and peace.

I hug him and make my way back into the house.

James is still standing on the patio talking to Lyn, but I can tell he's getting edgy.

His arms are crossed and his smile is stiff.

He rocks back and forth, shifting his weight from foot to foot.

"James," I call to him. "Shall I get you back to the RV? I'm sure your puppy needs attention."

He's relieved to see me.

He quickly hugs my Sister goodbye in an effort to seem normal and then says goodbye to everyone else.

"I'll drop you off and come back," I say to James. "The boys want Aunty Coco to share a new story with them and then tuck them in."

I busy myself hugging everyone goodbye and reassure the boys that I'll be right back.

"Thanks for the getaway," James mutters as he drives towards the RV park.

"What do you mean?" I ask innocently, knowing that every time he had the attention of my Siblings he found something to pick at them about. "You seemed like you were having a good time. I knew you had enough under the circumstances and that we should go when the going was good. Give them time to talk," I say.

I feel empowered and in control.

I feel refreshed.

*I can do this!*

*I have to in order to make this breakaway clean and safe for everyone.*

He suddenly punches the steering wheel.

"Your fucking family," his says, his voice is mocking and agitated, "never asked once how I was. It's always about them. They don't fucking care either. All they do is talk about themselves!" He speeds up to pass a minivan.

"What are you talking about?" I fired back at him. "We agreed to let the evening be about them tonight. Are you forgetting that? It wasn't about you."

"It has always been like that, Colleen. Always about them!"
We pull up in front of the RV and he slams the vehicle into park.
"Oh, get over yourself!" I spew, fed up with his rages. "When did
you EVER care? With all your lying, drinking, and cheating on
me, why would you let what my family does bother you one little
bit? You never wanted any of us anyway! They have done nothing
BUT try to accept you! It's YOU who have neglected US!"
I slam the truck door and stomp to the RV.
I unlock the door and quickly step inside.
He's right on my tail.
I can feel the heat of his rage creep up my back.
"You're such a self-righteous bitch!" he says. "Your whole self-
righteous family! You gloat about how good you are, how close you
are, and here's another part of your perfect family breaking up and
falling apart."
I turn and hit him in the chest.
He freezes.
I hit him again.
I grab his shirt and back him against the stairway.
I am surprised that my thinning, five foot three, hundred-and-five-
pound frame could push his five-foot-nine, hundred-and-ninety-
pound sack of used-to-be muscle.
His hands are in the air in an attempt not to strike back.
They are never his choice of weapon.
He chooses words.
Words and his self-serving manipulative mind.
He turns his face away from me as though I disgust him.
"You wouldn't know family, James!" I say through gritted teeth.
"You have had one all this time and never recognized love, nor
family, ALL THIS TIME!"
I release my hands from his shirt and press them firmly against
his chest.
I feel the heat of his skin and I feel his heart racing.

I feel a surge of grief and loss and hate and anger towards this man, this patient.

"You have had kindness and hope, laughter and joy in your hands and you didn't see it," I say. "You had the innocent, trusting love of two little children all this time and you didn't receive it! You spat on us and used us as your ruse to be seen as a family man! You hate my family because they can see through you and still try to love you! You only understand what YOU feel, what YOU want, and what YOU need! You expect everyone to make an effort for you, but when the going gets tough, you'd rather dispose of us than support us! As for saying my Children's names, I don't want YOU to say THEIR names ever again! You don't have the right."

I shove myself away from him.

His arms drop to their sides in defeat.

"I pity you and thank you at the same time." I step back, away from his scent that used to weaken my knees but now only weakens my stomach.

"You thank me?" he asks sarcastically.

"Yes. Because I know we, my Children and I, gave everything to this marriage and it was not us who betrayed it. WE will come out of this clean and clear of guilt. So thank you."

I step around him.

I take the truck keys from the side table where he dropped them and leave to spend the evening with my family.

# CHAPTER 16

## A Deal with God

*"Just because we are told
we have to go through others of authority to get to Him,
doesn't mean we have to."*
– Colleen Songs

Rising early to go for a run,
I reflect on the past evening.
I feel recharged from being with my family,
the ones who love me unconditionally and who know
what's happening,
focusing on the boys and their night time routine of stories
and laughter
and snuggles
and warmth.
I focused on them and let my reality fade into a sweet gentle
reprieve for my heart.
I swallowed back tears with each memory of tucking my
own Children into bed and our nights of lullabies and ani-
mated storytelling.
Driving back to the R.V. I prayed that with each hug and kiss of my
great-nephews somehow my own Children had a warm feeling and
memory pop into their hearts.
Feeling how much love I have for them.
Feeling that I am thinking about them right then and there too.
The campground is peaceful this morning.
The gated grounds give me ample distance to run.
Before I start jogging, I notice a small library and decide to peek in.
Loving books, I wonder if I can find a new one to sink my mind
into while embarking upon the next phase of my journey.
I enter the cozy white room.
The sitting areas of flowered "grandma" furniture and doily-clad
tables make the room inviting.
I see a computer in one corner of the room.
A thought whispers to my mind:
*Send an e-mail to the kids,*
*it is time to let them know.*
I'm suddenly scared as hell and my heart races.
*If he finds me I am dead and he will call the kids and hurt them more.*

I try to move but I'm frozen to the floor.

I breathe and try and evaluate where I am, if he can see me, how much time I have.

*I have to believe it will be okay and trust my gut feeling.*

*Learn from the past.*

I feel myself flying to the computer.

I start up the computer according to the steps specified on the little blue sticky note taped to the bottom of the screen.

I feel free and alive and empowered!

*My darlings! Momma's coming home.*

I log into my webmail account and see dozens of e-mails that I haven't been able to get to because he's kept me from using the laptop.

*Maybe someone will start wondering why I haven't replied.*

I click "Compose" and enter both Children's e-mail addresses.

I copy their Dad on the message.


"Dear Sissy and Andrew,

I'm so sorry. There are things I tried to save you from and things I didn't believe you were strong enough to handle. I should have had more faith. I should have never separated us. I went back on my promise that nothing ever would. When everything seemed out of control, I could no longer think clearly. All I could feel was the need to have you in a safe place.

Sissy, Momma loves you! I'm so sorry! I took you from our home instead of removing him from it! I should never have let you go. I just needed you safe! My beautiful daughter! How I long to hold you! You should never ever have been allowed to feel all this pain! You must feel abandoned by your Momma!

Andrew, know there isn't a day that I don't think about you.
You must feel ashamed and let down by your Momma too!
You are witnessing what is happening. My tender heart!
My Sonshine!

You have both been so brave! Too brave! You should never
have had to be so brave all these years!

I wish I could take it back. I wish I had said no to James and
none of us would be apart. We'd be living close to your Dad
and happy all this time. My heart aches for the mistakes I've
made. I, no WE, tried so hard to make this work with James.
I was so afraid of having another broken marriage, but in
that quest to build a secure home for us, it became more and
more unsafe until I no longer knew how to keep it together.

Know that James is very sick. None of this is you! Mom is
stronger. I know what needs to be done and I need you safe
at your dad's. My Babies, my Children, I love you!

Please call Aunty Mae. Call her and talk to her soon. She will
be my voice until I can get away. I'm coming home soon.

I love you, my darlings! Please still love your Momma. Xoxo"

I realize I've been holding my breath as I type.
I release my breath slowly to try and calm my racing heart.
I feel a huge weight lift off my heart, but as I go to push "Send" I
feel a hand on mine.
*God, no!!! Please, please, please!*
Tension binds my throat.
I push the chair back from the desk and stand to look into
James' eyes.
His stare is calm and steady.
His once vibrant blue eyes have turned to smoke.

He leads me to the door.

"Go for your run," he orders quietly while walking me outside.

He locks himself inside the library and stands at the window as I walk away.

I take a few steps and turn to look through the window.

He's at the computer.

I run.

I run.

I run.

I run on the beach with the sand sifting in my shoes.

I stop and fumble with the laces to take them off.

As soon as the skin of my feet touch the sand, I cry.

*From dust we come and to dust we will return.*

*Fuck!*

*Why did I pause?*

*I did not push send.*

*I did not push send!*

*I did not log out!*

*He is in my e-mail!*

*Stupid, stupid, stupid!*

*He is e-mailing my Children but not with my words.*

*Please know it is not Momma!*

*Please, please hear the words I tried to send you.*

*My Children!*

I sit in the sand.

I hug my knees to my chest.

I cry onto my knees.

If he didn't know already he knows now that I am planning to go home.

"Fine," I whisper to a God who seems so distant.

"Fiiiiiiine!" I wipe my face with the bottom of my t-shirt.

I talk to God as though he's standing right there in front of me.

"You want us to come to you as little children? As though you are the 'perfect father' and a 'safe place' for children to approach? Well then, Buddy, I'll make you a deal. You protect my Children from my patient's words and any more pain and I'll protect him, Your child, until I get him to a place where he's content long enough for me to get to Jayne's. Then he's all Yours. Even though he is your responsibility, for some reason I must carry this burden for you. I just want to get back to my life. If this is my punishment for loving him, for leaving my Children, then I will pay it. But You protect my Children!"
I brush the sand off.
*I am so sick of this emotional shit.*
I pick up my shoes and walk back to the RV.
He's there,
waiting.
I enter the Fifth Wheel and go straight to the shower, closing all doors behind me.
I need to get ready for the day.
We had promised Mae a day at the pier in White Rock with the boys and I must look refreshed.
The patient says nothing to me.
His smug look says he's in control.
*Condescending,*
*control-freaking*
*asshole!*
*I imagine he changed my password and rewrote my letter to say whatever the voices in his head told him to say.*
I send thoughts to my Children as hot water runs over my body.
*Feel the words that I wrote to you,*
*brush off the words that he wrote to you.*
*Know the difference in your heart of hearts.*
*Know I am coming home and that you are protected.*
*Mom made a deal,*
*a deal with God.*

# CHAPTER 17

## The Cookie Tin

*"I wrote a note and tucked it under the layer of wax paper:*
*'My husband has drugs in a baggy in the freezer.*
*I want to go home to my Children in Alberta.*
*He's suicidal.*
*I need help."*
— Colleen Songs

We are supposed to stay a week on the coast of British Columbia to wait out the time period before our international medical coverage kicks in.

I am supposed to attend my great-nephew's wedding before the patient and I go to the States.

But three days in one spot and he's ready to cross the border.

*It's all about him.*

It is nearing our five-year anniversary.

*Or has it already passed?*

I don't know.

I'm numb to the sentimentalities of our marriage.

We're approaching the Highway 99 border crossing into the States.

He doesn't know I left a note in the cookie tin that I put in the RV fridge freezer.

Last night I baked cookies to bring to Mae's boys today for another great adventure together, but before bed, he announced that he wanted to cross the border and start travelling south, even before our medical coverage allowed us to.

My stomach flipped, and my face reddened from the let-down, but I remained silent.

I quietly cleaned the kitchen from my baking.

He went to bed.

*You just do not want me spending any more time with Mae for fear something will be questioned.*

Fear began to creep into my knees, my stomach:

fear to be out of Canada again,

fear to be away from my Children,

fear I would never see them again,

and fear that I couldn't pull off this escape and live through it.

*You made a deal and God is supposed to stand by His word.*

I put the cookies in a tin.

*Yeah, but he pulled out of deals before and left me holding the bag.*

*I don't want to cross that border!*
I fear being in another country so far away again from
my Children.
I wrote a note and tucked it beneath the layer of wax paper, "My
husband has drugs in a baggy in the freezer. I want to go home to
my Children in Alberta. He's suicidal. I need help."
He was already asleep.
I wasn't exactly lying.
He keeps a little baggy of marijuana in the freezer for the odd
occasion when he needs to calm down, like after a rage or being
too drunk to pack up and leave.
I finished cleaning and then went to bed, imagining what would
happen when we reached the border crossing tomorrow.
Delighted with myself, I prayed for courage to see the
plan through.
*I may be home sooner than I think.*
I slept better that night than I had in weeks.


The border crossing isn't very busy.
There are two rigs ahead of us and a couple of passenger vehicles.
My stomach is doing leaps.
I try to cover my anxiety through slow breathing as I gaze at the
scenery around us.
The puppy yelps out the window, keeping James occupied as he
tries to soothe him.
*Thank you, Puppy, for your well-timed intervention.*
*I am grateful for you after all.*
Two U.S. border patrol officers approach us,
one on either side of our truck.
I smile and roll my window down.
I hand over my passport and the puppy's certificates.
*Shit!*
*I should have put the note in with the puppy's certificates!*

He's too young to be vaccinated and the officers reassure me that he should be okay in the States.

The officer standing on my side of the vehicle takes off his sunglasses and asks me to take off mine.

I make eye contact and smile.

"Hi, Mrs. Edwards," he says. "Where are you headed?"

"We're on our way to Arizona for my husband to seek some medical treatments," I fib.

*I'm not lying in theory.*

*I just know he has no intention of actually going through with the treatments.*

"Where exactly in Arizona?" he asks.

"Phoenix," I answer. "They have alternative medical treatment centres there."

He hands me a list of items to read through.

"Do you have anything on this list that needs to be claimed or discarded before crossing?" he inquires. "You cannot have anything that isn't in its original packaging nor produce that is not grown in the U.S."

He looks at me, trying to read my response.

"Oh." I'm getting nervous now as I feel the opportunity arise to pull the pin on this ruse.

*This is it!*

"We just stopped at a fruit stand, and I made a fresh batch of cookies last night. They are in the blue tin in the fridge. They're pretty good; you may want to confiscate them for sure!"

I smile and wait for his reply.

My heart races in anticipation.

The patient is busy: the puppy is crawling all over him while he tries to talk to the other officer.

They're not paying any attention to me.

*Dear Puppy, you are sooo getting any treat you want when we make it out of here!*

The officer is quietly contemplative as he holds my stare.

I'm sure he hears my heart pounding.

*Oh please hear my heart pounding.*

"Ma'am, will you go collect the produce and bring it in to the office, please."

He steps back to allow me to get out of the truck.

James looks over but he can't say anything as he's still talking with the other officer.

"Of course, Officer," I say, "but I do need to reach into the console for the RV keys."

He nods and watches me as I reach for the keys and step out of the truck to make my way into the RV.

"Just the produce, Ma'am; the baked goods are fine," he issues kindly.

I feel my face redden as I open the door.

*Crap!*

*Now what?*

*I need you to follow me!*

I turn to look at him before going on.

"Are you sure?" I ask. "You are welcome to step in and see if there's anything else we need to declare."

He smiles. "That's all right. We'll be checking the storage bins only. We'll get your husband to open them for us."

*Jesus!*

*You're dumb!*

*So much for all the news about how anal you guys are!*

*I could have ten guns in here and a load of drugs and get away with it!*

*You should be fired!*

I step inside and proceed to gather the apples and pears.

*Damn it!*

*Why did I not think to put the note in these bags?*

*Stupid, stupid, stupid!*

*Now what?*

"Ma'am?" The officer steps inside while checking things off on his clipboard.

"Yes?" I turn to him with my arms full of fruit, hoping he'll ask to look in the fridge.

"Is that everything?" the officer asks.

"Yes, this is all the produce. Do you need to see anywhere else?"

*Oh please ask to see anywhere else for fuck's sake!*

"That is fine, Ma'am. You can follow me to the compost bins, then to the office, please." He steps out of the Fifth Wheel and helps me down the stairs, closing the door behind me.

I follow him to the office after I dump the produce in the compost bin.

I don't see the patient or the other officer anywhere.

I go inside the building and there's the patient, standing by the counter with the other officer, smiling and talking about travelling with a puppy.

The patient looks at me and smiles as I approach the counter.

"How's everything?" I ask as lightly as I can despite wanting to scream.

"It's good. The officer was just telling me about his puppy. It's a bulldog." The patient is jovial and my stomach turns thinking about Wyatt and how I miss him.

My memory flashes images of the dog chasing the Children, hearing the kids laugh,

seeing them run and play peekaboo in the trees.

"Where's the ladies' room?" I ask a man behind the counter, stone-faced, as I can no longer fake this smile.

*I'm so pissed off!*

He points to the hallway behind me and I immediately follow the direction of his finger.

I lock myself in the bathroom and allow the frustrated tears to fall.

I turn on the tap and let the water run to cover up my crying.

*God, what am I to do now?*

*I want to get back to my Children.*

*You promised me!*

I take a few deep breaths and repeat our deal to the image in the mirror.

"You protect my Children from his words and any more pain and I'll protect Your child until I get him to a place where he's content long enough for me to get to Jayne's."

I feel a swarm of doubt rise over me.

I feel a touch of guilt as I realize I almost went back on my part of the bargain.

*I do not know if I have the strength to see this through, God!*

*I do not know if I can do it!*

*We're going to have some serious words if I don't make it home!*

I cry a few more sobs, releasing the tension from my head, my face, my neck, my shoulders.

I splash my face with the icy cold water running in the sink.

I look at myself in the mirror.

I breathe in the courage of my Mother,

the strength of my Sisters,

the subliminal plea

from my Children

for their Momma to come back to them.

I remember once again the scripture that says God never gives us more than we can handle.

"Frig, you're one strong woman if that's the case!" I say to myself.

The mirror smiles back weakly.

"You've come this far; let's go get him settled and you'll be on your way."

I pat my face dry and make my way back to the counter where I left the patient.

I know my face is puffy and red and I don't care.

Both the patient and the officers look at me.

*Pretend to have some feminine weakness.*

"Just feeling a little queasy, boys," I lie with a smile. "I always get a little carsick travelling."

*You're all idiots.*

"We can head out," the patient says. "Everything's fine."

He places his hand on my back.

I try not to shirk it off.

"Thank you, officers," I say, but they're already busy with the next drivers.

The patient and I get back to the truck and he starts it up.

He's quiet.

The puppy is asleep on my seat so I pick him up and put my little hero on my lap for the first time.

*I remember what you tried to do for me, distracting him as I hinted to the dumb border dude.*

*Sorry it didn't work out as I had planned.*

*I am not so good at tricking people,*

*not like he is.*

*And I don't want to become like he is.*

We drive through the gates and pick up speed.

We're back in the United States.

I feel the miles between my Children and I growing again.

I close my eyes and send them a silent prayer.

"Want a cookie?" the patient asks me.

"What?" I reply, startled.

"Want a cookie?" he repeats. "I brought them in so we can eat while we drive. They're behind me on the seat. Will you grab them?"

He is calm and cheerful.

I reach for them and open the lid.

The note is not there.

"You're a mental cunt, Colleen. Maybe it's you who needs help," he says. "Did you even think of what that note might have done to me?"

He smiles.

He fucking smiles and reaches out for a cookie.

# CHAPTER 18

## Morning Prayer

*"I place a hand on each knee and I breathe
so deeply that I am breathing for all three of us.
I exhale the distance between us.
I inhale life.
I exhale him."*
— Colleen Songs

The days slip by with every mile we pull down the western coast of the United States.

No place is good enough to stay.

Either there's no satellite service,

no cell service,

no gym good enough,

no pool big enough.

It's raining.

It's too hot.

There's not enough shade.

It's too isolated.

It's too populated.

He is restless and miserable.

I don't bother to ask him why, because I really don't care.

I'm a person who usually hates to swear but I curse on a dime every waking moment.

I no longer know what day it is.

I only feel my legs and back aching from the continual driving and stopping at rest stops for a few hours of sleep.

In Idyllwild, California we finally arrive at an RV Resort qualified enough for him to finally settle.

*Hallafuckinlooyah*!

We pull into the resort and make camp.

I'm shaky and exhausted and the first thing I do is lay down on the sofa bed, my evening oasis, and sleep.

I sleep and I sleep.

Once in a while I awaken to the odd noise of James making himself food or watching TV or stepping in and out of the RV to have a cigarette or walk the puppy.

I drift back to sleep not caring that he doesn't care how long I'm asleep.

I wake up and think it must be morning as I hear the sound of the coffee maker.

It doesn't perk me up.

I feel listless and less than alive.

I don't want to talk to him nor see him but I get up to wash my
face and get dressed.

The patient is sitting in the living room,

rocking in his stupid chair.

*I am going to burn that chair one day.*

I don't make eye contact with him.

I make my coffee 'to-go' in my favourite travel mug:

two teaspoons of Demerara sugar

and a splash of cream.

I stir until I no longer feel the grit of the sugar against the spoon.

I tap the spoon on the lip of the mug,

screw on the lid,

walk towards the door,

open it and step down onto the orange-coloured gravel blanketing
the campsite.

I'm barefoot and the ground is already warm.

I step back into the RV to search for my shoes.

He continues to rock in his chair.

He's no longer watching the television.

He's watching me.

I can't find my shoes anywhere:

no running shoes,

no sandals.

*You have GOT to be kidding me.*

I look at him.

He continues rocking in his chair,

staring at me,

amused with that smug smile on his face I loathe.

"Fuck yourself!" I reply in answer to his amusement.

*He thinks that if he takes my shoes he can keep me here.*

*That is NOT what is keeping me here, you fucking idiot.*

I step back out onto the gravel and start my walk.

My feet hurt with every step.

The crushed rocks sting my soles, but I'm more pissed off than in pain.

So I walk.

I walk

and I walk.

The pain begins to dissipate as the gravel softens to sand.

I climb the long driveway and encourage myself to breathe deeper.

The sun comforts my face.

I begin to take notice of the vista that surrounds me.

I feel myself being drawn out of the rolled-up ball hiding in my belly and back into my limbs.

I find myself a place to sit overlooking the valley.

Yellow, sun-kissed grasses softly wave to the oddly spaced clusters of pine trees towering above them.

Lonely, abandoned boulders scatter over the rolling hills beneath my feet.

Tufts of tiny cacti peek around the shadows of the boulders, wanting to be touched but knowing they're cursed to prick anyone who dares to caress them.

*Such a lonely life for such a beautiful little thing.*

I sit on one of the boulders.

A thought passes through my mind of my becoming like the cacti, biting anyone who dares to come near me.

It's hot from the sun.

I welcome the sting on my aching hips and make myself comfortable.

I sip my coffee and breathe.

I close my eyes and breathe.

I hear the mournful cry of a hawk in the distance.

The ache of its tone is lonely and resonates with my own heart song.

I imagine my Children sitting with me, exploring the trails;

my Son, taking in the scenery with his deep silent thoughts;
my Daughter, debating which hillside would challenge her
daring curiosity.
I cross my legs and set my coffee aside.
I place a hand on each knee and I breathe so deeply that I'm
breathing for all three of us.
I exhale the distance between us.
I inhale life.
I exhale him.
I inhale hope.
I exhale defeat, for I will not be defeated.
I inhale my Daughter's heart opening.
I exhale doubt that she can hear me.
I inhale my Son's heart opening.
I exhale doubt that he can hear me.
And then I pray…

*Sissy, hear your Momma.*
*Andrew, hear your Momma.*
*I am coming home to heal us.*
*I am coming home to free us.*
*You are strong and wise.*
*He can no longer hurt you.*
*I am stronger and wiser.*
*He can no longer hurt me.*

*I had to leave to protect you.*
*But Momma's coming home.*
*Please hear me, my Children.*
*I know you can.*

*I know you can feel me.*
*I am entering your thoughts right now.*

*I am pulling at your heart strings.*
*I am attaching them to mine.*

*He cannot separate us.*
*You are of me.*
*I am of you.*
*I love you.*

*You'll know everything soon.*
*Know your Momma loves you.*
*Love is all that matters.*
*I am on my way home.*
*Momma loves you.*

I open my eyes and I feel in my heart of hearts that they've heard me.

If in this very moment they feel sad, or they think about me, I know that my message reached them.

*We are all but only one thought away from one another,*
*only one belief away.*

I pick up my coffee cup and place my feet back on the ground.

The sand is hot as I tiptoe around the debris of leaves and bristles that I didn't notice before.

I make my way back down the hill to the RV.

The sand turns to pebbles.

Mother Nature no longer cushions my steps.

*I must hold up my end of the bargain on my own.*

*Thanks for the break.*

The pebbles turn to gravel.

I stumble my way to our campsite.

I see that he's standing outside smoking a cigarette, watching me pick my way back to the Fifth Wheel.

*I never want to see another Fifth Wheel again as long as I live.*

I open the outside panel of the RV where we keep a small bucket.
I grab it,
fill it with water,
and place it beside the picnic table.
I sit down and soak my tenderized feet.
*I am strong.*
*I am well.*
*I can do this.*

# CHAPTER 19

## One Last Good Time

*"There is no greater loneliness than being alone WITH someone."*
– Colleen Songs

The next two weeks are incredibly quiet.
I find all my shoes stashed under the cubby of the stairs to
the bedroom.
I put them in a bin inside the sofa bed cubby where I sleep.
I assume he is feeling his loss of control over me and is therefore
attempting to try and regain control.
I chalk it up to his being ill and do not let it anger me further.
Instead I choose pleasantry:
long spells of book-reading,
walks,
workouts,
and song writing.
Idyllwild allows me to be idle for awhile.
He's pleasant and leaves me alone to do my own thing as he goes
about doing what makes him content.
His everyday world is sunbathing,
swimming,
getting back into working out,
watching the news,
drinking,
and smoking while rocking in his chair.
That's about it.
I am not questioning the delay in our stay.
We have time before his treatments start, so if this is what he needs
I just let him have it.
I've developed my own pattern for peace in my life.
But each day I wake up lonely,
and for the first time I really notice it:
loneliness.
Though I'm not alone,
I am.
I read once that there's no greater loneliness than being alone
WITH someone.

I've been wearing that denial of truth like a cloak of security and protection against the cold that I'm living in.

I don't need intimacy and love.

I no longer trust love anyway.

I don't need a man in my life.

I don't WANT a man in my life.

I can be happy without sharing my life with someone.

It's much safer that way.

I wrap myself in that cloak and I'm okay.

I can do anything.

But no matter what I do now, the cloak feels tattered and heavy.

I push aside the mournful feeling it leaves me with and simply try not to think about what a warm hand would feel like on my skin.

I try not to yearn for a mind that listens to me,

shares with me,

and rejoices without chains.

The days float by.


Today we leave Idyllwild and I am a little sad.

It has been my home for the longest period of time since leaving home.

Two sweet solid weeks.

I've made no friends here for fear of their seeing through me, and for fear of hearing the questions I fear most…

"How could a mother leave her Children?"

"What are YOU doing with HIM?"

"Why are you with him?"

"Why don't you just go?"

"What kind of mother are you?"

I have no one here who I will miss, just my routine and the quiet.

The patient's next destination is Phoenix, Arizona and the clinics where he has made appointments.

And as we still have a few weeks to go he wants to make some stops along the way.

He's positive about getting the help he needs to get better.

A part of me aches for him to be well – not from missing him, but rather for his own peace.

I hold no hope for him to be who he once was,

if he ever really was that person I first met.

I don't think he was ever healthy for me and my Children.

A check-list item we don't think about when considering someone as our mate:

'Is he healthy for me?'

This should be a top-of-the-list item for anyone seeking a life partner.

I know that now.

As we pack the RV for the next leg of the trip, I think about Wayne and our last trip together.


We travelled to Wayne's aunt's very formal wedding in Saskatoon.

I was actually able to buy a formal gown and I was going to sing a song that I wrote for them.

While they were just beginning their journey of being husband and wife, our marriage was so over.

Wayne and I were simply awaiting the sale of our property.

We were already making plans to move on.

Our Children were young and adorable.

If any two parents loved and adored their Children before themselves, it's Wayne and me.

Wayne didn't want us to be over but my heart knew it was.

It was hard to mask our anxiety and broken-hearted questions that we asked ourselves, and one another, often:

"How can I hurt my best friend?"

"He's SUCH a nice guy; why can't I love him anymore?"

"Why doesn't she love me anymore?"

"How can I split up my family and still be calm and loving?"

"He doesn't want anyone else to be their father."

"I don't want anyone else to be their mother."

Three years of trying to make things work while living separated in the same house is not something I would recommend for anyone.

We were wearing each other thin.

When we arrived in Saskatoon and had settled into our hotel room, we argued over what we wanted to do next.

I wanted him to do whatever his family needed him to do.

He wanted to spend time with us, together as a family.

I asked him if he was sure.

I told him that I didn't mind staying in the room with the kids while giving him the freedom to be with his family during this special time.

It had always been an issue before: his limited time with his own family.

We argued and argued about the next few hours.

I tried to set him free for this occasion.

He tried to keep the last threads of our family together for this occasion.

The day's heat added to the tension.

He got angry and smacked me in the forehead, "Get some sense in that pea brain of yours, would you, and hear me!"

His classic reaction of frustration:

calling me down.

I started crying and rubbed my forehead.

This smack was a little harder than usual.

The Children started crying.

We placated our Children's sobbing questions by saying, "Oh, Mommy and Daddy were not hearing each other."

"Grownups make mistakes too, but we're sorry. We promise to listen better."

We hugged them and they settled down.

We promised them, "We will learn to listen better to what the other person is trying to say."

We cuddled them, we laughed, and we made a resolution.

We said, "This is just silly! It's so hot we're grumpy. Let's run a bath and have fun."

Wayne ran a bath and settled the Children into the tub and they played and played.

I ran around for towels and toys and snacks and fresh clothes.

The Children laughed and poured water over Wayne's head.

I saw his shoulders shake softly with every bucketful.

I knew he was crying.

I knew his heart was breaking.

My heart broke knowing I was hurting my dear, sweet friend.

I joined in on the fun and leaned over the tub for the Children to pour water over my head too.

I put my hand over Wayne's and took in the giggles and laughs and we played until the Children wanted to stop.

I promised to just let all of our heartache go for the sake of our peace and this family occasion.

This one last time I would give us everything we wanted to be: a family that will never break up.

We may be apart after we go home, but we'll never break apart.

Right then I decided that I was just going to have fun,

one last good time,

for him,

for me,

for us,

for the beautiful Children we would never have had without one another.

We had so much fun that weekend and the wedding was a blast.

My song was a hit.

We danced and laughed and my mind said, "To hell with it!"

Wayne let go and had fun.

I saw him as my friend, laughing again.
I was still in-like with my friend.
I wasn't in-love with the husband.
We simply didn't fit.
The trip home was fun too.
We allowed our resolve to carry us home.
It led us to a peaceful night once we got there,
tucking in the Children with fond memories,
and hugging one another in gratitude
for one more beautiful memory.

As I finish packing up the RV, a sense of calm comes over me.
*What are you trying to tell me?*
I keep doing what I'm doing, a little slower, a little more aware of
the senses that are surrounding me.
Then I understand.
*Just let go.*
*You are going home soon.*
*Make this last trip peaceful.*
I'm a little ticked at myself for thinking this way.
This is a totally different situation.
*Am I just being too nice again?*
It's not like when Wayne, the Children, and I went to the wedding.
*Wayne was not a selfish, all-about-me, controlling, sick asshole who manipu-*
*lated me away from my Children!*
I'm arguing with my silent self, frustrated with my feelings
and thoughts.
I shove the awning pull into the side cubby of the RV and slam the
door closed, twisting the latch hard.
"Hey!" the patient exclaims, "be careful."
He comes to inspect the door.
*SEE! He cares more about a thing than he does about me.*
*I am not going to give HIM one last good time.*

*There.*

*This subliminal debate is over.*

I turn away and feel my body tense.

I'm offended at the thought of this even being close to what happened with Wayne and me.

However I am not fully UNaware of my repeated habit of giving too much.

*It is not just for the patient,*

*it is for you.*

My thoughts succumb to the messages these memories offer me.

I get it now.

I breathe in and turn to look at him.

He's scowling at me.

"Sorry," I say. "I was lost in my own thoughts. I guess I don't know my own strength."

My attempt at humour doesn't work, but he doesn't make any nasty remarks either.

He heads for the truck.

I let it go.

And I do it for me.

# CHAPTER 20

## Tombstone

*"He is smiling and enjoying being out of the present and into the past,*
*free of the burden,*
*free of his mind."*
— Colleen Songs

Another hot day.

I wake up sweaty.

My head is thick from deep sleep and I'm still tired.

We drove from Idyllwild straight through to Tucson, Arizona, over six hundred and sixty kilometres and close to seven hours of road time.

This is our next stop on the way to the patient's appointments in Phoenix.

We have three weeks to go.

It's dark when we arrive at the gated campground in Tucson, adjacent to an RV dealership so that we can get supplies and maintenance done on the Fifth Wheel.

He wants everything touched up that bothered him about the RV along the way.

He needs it off his mind so he can focus on his treatments.

I breathe myself awake.

The sofa bed is taking a toll on my back.

I'm stiff and my muscles feel bruised.

Long slow breaths,

long slow stretches,

I roll over and ease myself slowly out of bed.

Some days I wake up expecting an MS flare-up with all the stress I've been under, but for some reason it stays at bay.

I am grateful for this but very aware that it may hit hard once I'm finally away from the stress and in a safe place.

I yawn and stretch one more time as I sit on the side of the bed attempting to waken.

The patient rocks in his chair across from me, sipping his morning coffee.

He smiles.

"Good morning," I say quietly.

"I have an idea," he says cheerfully.

"Hold on," I whisper and find my way to the bathroom to pee,
wash my face,
comb my hair,
ready myself for my morning run.
I haven't seen the campground in daylight so I'm hoping to find
somewhere to jog.
Any pathway will do.
I pour myself some coffee and sit on the sofa bed across from him.
"What's your idea?" I ask, drinking my coffee.
I'm not sure what to expect, but I'm ready now for just
about anything.
"Well, I called the RV dealership and they can come and pick
up the RV this morning," he offers lightly. "It'll take a couple
of days to do the work I want so I thought we could go to
Tombstone again."
He seems pleased with himself.
*He looks bright and alive this morning.*
I take another sip and ponder his idea.
Tombstone is where the most famous shootout of the Wild West,
the Gunfight at the O.K. Corral, took place in 1881.
One thing we had in common was our love of history.
The patient and I had taken a trip there a couple of years before,
during Christmas break.
He brought me there to cheer me up as the Children wanted to
have Christmas with their Dad that year.
We had so much fun.
We met a couple of the actors, Jake and Matt, who performed in
re-enactments of the shootout.
They were so sweet and fun and let us join in on an act
at the Crystal Palace Saloon after the show, a gift for the
patient's birthday.
*Oh, what the heck.*
*I would love to see Tombstone again.*

"Sure," I surrender, though I'm exhausted and in need of rest after yet another long drive.

*One last good time.*

"If that will make you happy, I'm for it," I say. "I would like to go for my run first. I need to get the soreness out of me."

I have another sip of coffee.

"We have time," says the patient. "You go and I'll get things ready."

He's excited and seems almost normal.

*This is a nice morning.*

A part of me wants to be happy.

*It is purely a moment,*

*but I will take it.*

I drink one last sip of coffee and prepare for my run.

I find my runners and a pair of socks.

I step outside and sit down on the steps to put on my gear as I observe the campground; a perfectly groomed and paved parking lot.

Huge stalls are separated by small gardens with fire pits neatly welcoming each camper.

My path this morning will consist of weaving through the paved lanes until I can no longer think.

*This is all I need to carry on for another day.*

I lose count of my laps.

It soon becomes unbearably hot so I make my way back to the Fifth Wheel to get ready for our drive to Tombstone.

I notice that my heart is lighter when I think of going back there.

I make my way back to the RV to shower, dress, and pack for the drive to Tombstone.

*It will be nice to see Jake and Matt again.*

The patient busies himself by making all the arrangements for the dealership to pick up the RV.

It's a welcome break not to have to help prep the RV for pick up.

After such a long drive and only one night's sleep to recover, I've simply had enough of that routine.

I throw some basics in a bag, grab a little red bandana for Puppy's Western apparel of choice, and get us both in the truck.
Puppy nestles into his spot on the console.
Tombstone.
A quaint old Western town, popular with tourists all year long, full of legends and stories about gamblers and wranglers, sheriffs and outlaws.
We're going during a busy time: 'Helldorado Days', a celebration of Tombstone's history.
Rooms will be hard to find in town but thankfully we find a spot at the Best Western for the first night that provides us with two beds.
We'll move to our friend Craig's motel for the remainder of the weekend.
We discovered it on the last night of our last visit and promised to go back there to stay and support his business whenever we returned.
Sparse vegetation, cacti, sand, dust, and tumbleweeds set within a wide valley surrounded by ragged hills call out to me.
*What a breakaway!*
I imagine stealing a horse and riding until nobody can find me.
*What would it have been like to ride like the wind where outlaws, ranchers, and cowboys rode and worked and drove cattle through such arid land?*
It was probably rough as hell, but I revel in the drama and romance of it all.
I lose myself in the daydream for a moment.
The patient and I spend the day walking around Tombstone.
We get an early night's sleep and arrive by late morning at Craig's motel, where we settle in and make plans for the day.
The puppy we generically named Buddy is content in the air-conditioned room.

After being fed and walked, we settle him into his crate and he
curls himself up to sleep.
We head into town, grateful that Craig and Matt, who also reside at
the motel, are animal lovers.
They promise to check in on Buddy once in a while.

We find our way down the dusty Main Street and are immediately
captivated by the events in town.
A gun show here,
a showdown there,
and the classic shootout
at the O.K. Corral.
So many people are dressed in period clothing.
The patient gets directions to a store where we can find costumes.
It's a moment of playfulness and I am able to forget my misery.
We stop to compliment an impeccably-dressed couple on
their apparel.
Plum satin and black lace adorn this full-figured lady in perfect
hand stitchery.
Her blonde hair is neatly coiffed in ribbons and swirls.
Pink cheeks decorate her pretty face where time is gifting her
softness of age.
Her escort is tall and lanky, debonair in his grey wool suit and
embroidered vest sparkling from the chain of a silver mine-era
pocket watch.
We chat with them and listen closely to their thick drawling
accents, trying to place where they're from.
We soon discover that the woman has designed and hand stitched
their heritage clothing.
The couple travels from re-enactment to re-enactment all over the
United States to participate in special historical events.
Once a bit of a seamstress myself, I'm fascinated.

We invite them to meet us at the saloon where Jake and Matt would be dealing the table where Wyatt Earp dealt the game of Faro when he first arrived in Tombstone.

They are thrilled to join us and want to film it.

We find the costumer and dive into the wide array of period clothing that she has in her store.

She dresses James in gunslinger gear, complete with a prop gun and holster.

I know exactly what I am looking for and waste no time in putting my ensemble together.

*Sharon Stone, bite me!*

I giggle to myself as I immerse myself back in time.

Jake is setting up and waiting for us.

His eyes grow big and friendly when he sees us coming.

I hug him tightly and tell him how nice it is to see him again.

He looks me up and down, laughing when I blush.

His big booming voice says how some women were shot for looking so beautiful back in the day.

I laugh.

My dress is a stunner.

Yards and yards of smoky grey satin sweep over my body as sheer black lace from bodice to waist creeps down to expose my navel. Lace caplet sleeves tease my sun-kissed shoulders as a black lace shawl and fingerless gloves offer finishing-touch shadows to this lady of the night.

"I think a lady must have gotten shot from the crossfire between you boys thinking it was all your decision who gets her," I coyly say, loving the attention and the part I'm playing.

We have a good laugh and he leads me to a chair beside him to play the part of the counter for the game.

"Now, just so you know," his booming voice warns, "counters also got shot on the spot for miscounting too."

He winks as he hands me an abacus and then pushes my chair in
for me as I shuffle the extra fabric of my dress around to avoid any
of its splendour getting torn beneath a chair leg.
I slowly pull the skirt of my gown up my right leg to discreetly
display the tiny pistol that the costumer slipped into my garter as
we headed out of her shop.
"No worries," I tap the pistol cheekily. "I can make a mouse dance.
I'm one step ahead of you, Sir."
With a hearty laugh Jake turns to greet the patient, who has already
been greeted by Matt at the bar.
After a few words, the patient and Matt make their way to the table
to join in the game.

Matt's across from me.
The patient is in the chair on my right.
He's smiling and enjoying being out of the present and into
the past.
He gives me no notice, totally enveloped in the game and being
with his friends.
*It is like he is free of burdens,*
*free of his mind.*
Our new friends arrive as we begin the game.
I introduce them to Matt and Jake, who is thrilled to have more
people around his table.
They set up their camera as Jake repeats the rules of the game and
each of our roles.
There's another bout of laughter as he deals everyone in.
I fall right into my part as the counter.
The game is fun and we play our roles as we imagine them to be.
We also ask Jake questions.
A born-and-raised Tombstonian, Jake tells us about the history
of the game, the 'local-truth' version of the Earps' presence in
Tombstone, and the shoot-out at the OK Corral.

I find I'm taking on a sweet Southern accent and so we make up a story about where I come from and how I afforded such a dress in this dusty town.

I'm escaping into a world of make believe and I feel my soul resting for a little while.

The evening is fun and cheery.

Jack Daniel's makes his way around and around the table as we play and laugh and gamble.

I'm teased about Jack making his way to my glass only once.

"I have to keep sharp," I say as I flick the abacus. "I don't want to get shot and spoil such a lovely dress that I worked so hard on my back for."

Everyone hoots with laughter as I pretend my way to the Oscars.

Then it's time for dinner.

Game over.

We all walk together to have dinner at a lovely café promising home-cooking and fine wine.

The crowds have thinned a bit during the dinner hour and we walk in a row down the centre of the street.

I feel that I really am Silver Sally from Savannah, Georgia, who made her fortune in silver from the miners' hard "labouring."

At this point, any dream of being touched thrills me, but not by James.

I look over to him and smile.

He does not even spare me a glance.

I sigh and continue my pace with my friends.

*Thank goodness I am just pretending.*

*I would be willing bait.*

As the evening turns to dusk, and our meal folds with our last sips of port, I feel myself tiring and in need of returning to our room to check on Buddy.

I need to get some rest before joining the group for evening drinks at the Crystal Palace.

I leave the patient amongst our friends and promise to return within the hour.

After letting Buddy out for a walk, I place him in his kennel and leave the door open for some fresh evening air.

I freshen up and check that my dress is still in perfect condition.

It's like I've stepped back in time when I see my reflection in the mirror.

*Very provocative, I must say.*

"Well, Sharon, this dress has yours beat," I tell myself in the mirror.

I turn to leave and jump at the sight of Craig standing in the doorway.

"That's a fine dress on you," he says, flattering me with a complimentary pearly white smile.


*Gosh, he really does look like Ty Pennington from that television show Extreme Home Makeover.*

I recall thinking that when I first met him.

Lack of touch from my husband led me to never miss watching that show.

*I'm pathetic.*

Amused by my own secret crushes throughout the years of loneliness, my heart flutters when I see Craig.

*I am crushing!*

He smiles and my knees soften.

"Oh, hi Craig!" I'm blushing and he's still smiling. "Oh. Uhm. Yeah, I'm just feeling the role in this dress," I say. "Going to join us at the Palace?"

"I'd love to but I have guests to tend to," he replies, openly disappointed with a playful pout on his very nice lips.

*Oh Colleen stop it!*

He turns to leave and then hesitates.

He asks me quietly if I'd like to see a special part of the motel.

That he doesn't show this part of his property to just anybody.

I giggle.

"That sounds like a proposition of questionable intentions," I purr playfully. "But I'd love to."

I don't lie.

*I do not care what he intends nor what he has to show me.*

*Married or not, just being in Craig's presence feels nice, especially after not having James's attention for so long.*

*It feels nice.*

I follow him to the side of the main entrance of the lobby, through a gate,

and into a rugged garden that's like a setting from an old Western movie.

He takes me to a classic hunter's cabin.

There is a rocking chair on the porch,

bits and pieces of timeless memorabilia,

tools and trinkets,

jugs and pots,

a picket fence,

and a weathered axe held hostage in a large chopping block waiting for someone strong enough to release it.

I'm enchanted.

I feel like I've stepped back in time.

I twirl around in my dress to take in every time-piece of this setting.

Craig stands in the gateway, smiling and watching me.

He's gorgeous,

sweet,

and kind.

"I saw you walking in and I just had to see you here," he shyly confesses, "in that dress. I want to take a picture but I'm not allowed to photograph this area because it's used for movies."

I feel like I'm in another world.

*Do not wake me up.*

*I do not want to wake up in my real world.*

"Thank you for sharing this with me," I say. "I won't tell a soul."

I smile at him.

"Thank you for this vision," he replies.

For a moment, my heart flutters.

*It has been so long and it feels so good.*

I walk towards him to find my way out of this secret place.

He steps back to let me pass through the gate, back to the main entrance.

"I'm just going to change," I excuse myself,

flustered,

blushing.

"I don't think I want anybody else seeing me in this dress now."

I pass by him.

*He smells so good.*

Craig walks toward his guests who are waiting for him in the courtyard by a very inviting fire.

I find my way back to my room.

# CHAPTER 21

## Staying the Course

⌒

*"I dream of being in a hidden garden,*
*lulled by arms that love me,*
*slipping his hands beneath my skirt."*
— Colleen Songs

I return to the room I share with the patient and close the door.
It takes me a few minutes to get out of the dress due to all the pins
it needed to hug my small frame.
I find myself fighting emotions I hadn't expected:
desire,

attraction,

captivity,

survival,

fear,

longing,

obligation.

*Do not read into things that you may only be thinking because your husband
has not touched you,*
*nor loved you*
*ever really.*
Tears burn my eyes.
*No one will know if anything were to happen tonight.*
*You have needs.*
*Anyone would understand.*
*Go be touched.*
*Go be desired.*
*You have liked him since you met him the first year you came here!*
*Who cares if it is just a fling or that he may not mean it the way you feel it.*
The dress is now at my feet and I turn to look in the mirror.
I touch myself.
I touch my hair.
I touch my face.
I touch my lips.
I touch my breasts.
I run my hands down my stomach towards my secret garden.
*What is wrong with you?*
*You are beautiful.*
*You are fit.*

*You are desirable.*
*Why does your husband not want you?*
*Why has he never really wanted you?*
Tears flow,
again.
Frustration builds and releases with each breath.
I step out of the dress and reach for other clothes to wear.
*You are not going to have a fling!*
*One day the kids would hear about it and you have messed up enough already.*
*Give yourself time.*
*This will all be history.*
*Get through this.*
*Make your way to Jayne's and then back home.*
*All will be well.*
I dress in a simple white blouse and skirt.
*So much cooler.*
I freshen up my makeup one more time.
I tell myself to be grateful that I still have the ability to blush.
*You were given a sweet moment.*
*Be grateful for it.*
I pick up Buddy and hold him for some kind of reciprocal
love connection.
I place him back in his kennel,
top up his food and water,
put down fresh paper,
blow him a kiss,
and walk to the saloon to meet my group for the promised
evening drinks.
I hate walking into a bar alone.
"Ladies never enter bars alone," my Mom would say.
My face is red as soon as I walk through the doors.
I don't see the patient anywhere.
I look around and see Jake talking to the bartender.

I quickly make my way to my friend and ask him where my
husband went.

He puts his arm around me protectively.

I look up into his huge eyes as he tells me that the patient left
with Matt.

I am offered a drink but I refuse.

I kiss his cheek and walk back to the motel in case I missed the
patient and he's angrily looking for me.

*I did take a little longer than I said I would be.*

When I arrive at the street across from the motel I notice the twirl-
ing red and blue lights of ambulance and police on the corner.

I stop and look around.

Craig is standing with his guests on the sidewalk in front of
the motel.

He notices me and walks over to meet me.

I tell him that I can't find my James or Matt.

I look at the ambulance and back at him as a horrible fleeting
thought passes through my mind that it may be James and Matt.

"It's not them," he says, reading my mind. "It's a couple who are
staying here. A drunk driver hit them as they were walking across
the road."

Tears well in his eyes.

I put my hand on his shoulder to comfort him.

"Come and sit down," I tell him softly.

He asks his guests to please make their way back to their rooms or
the courtyard.

Everyone is disturbed by the events, offering comfort and words
of disbelief.

Their fellow guests were killed so close to home,
one block from the safety of the motel.

I'm shaken and I don't even know them.

*The end of life stands only metres away from us.*

*Why does James want death so badly?*

I shake the thoughts from my head and search for a place to sit down.

I see that Craig is already sitting on the bench right outside my room door.

I go inside to get Buddy for something to hold, and then I sit next to my friend.

He is shaken from the events of losing his longtime guests just moments before.

His head sinks to his hands and his shoulders are trembling.

I lay my hand on his shoulder again, hoping it gives him some sort of comfort.

He takes my hand in his.

*I want to kiss him.*

*I really want to kiss him.*

*Very bad timing, Colleen.*

I sit quietly beside him, not really knowing what to feel and battling timing versus right and wrong.

*James will not even care.*

*He does not even love you.*

*He is out getting drunk.*

Craig keeps my hand in his.

I feel my heart tighten for his pain and for my misery.

"I'll go find Matt, okay?" I offer quietly. "You need your friend here."

I kiss his cheek.

He smells musky and warm.

I hug him around his shoulders and then stand up to leave.

"What are you doing with him?" he whispers.

I freeze.

"What are you doing with him?" he looks at me and asks again.

"What is a woman like you doing with a guy like him? You deserve better. Life is too short."

He shakes his head and places it back in his hands.

*I do not know what to say.*
This man sees through the act, the façade of a happily
married couple.
This man who doesn't know me other than as a visitor to his town
from two years ago, this man who is from another world than
mine, sees through me!
*How many have seen through the false front and said nothing?*
I feel a mixture of abandonment from my long-time friends, who
have never told me what they really think, and admiration for this
man who barely knows me but sees through me and cares enough
to tell me his true feelings.
"I don't know anymore, Craig," I admit. "I just know that I am
no better than he is on so many levels, I've let things happen that
made a mess of things. I see that now. Everything has a reason and
I probably won't know that reason until I leave. And I am going. I
just have to do things right. Not only for me, you see, but for my
Children too."
I want to tell him that I am leaving James as soon as I get him
settled into a routine with his appointments.
But I feel I don't need to;
that it wouldn't be safe to.
I certainly do not want to start anything with anybody.
*Can't trust it to be true anyway.*
I smile inside myself and feel lighter from my own revelations.
A weight is released from my chest.
I thank God for this Angel beside me who has helped me see my
own answers.
"I'll go find Matt, okay?" I whisper. "I'll be right back."
He nods and releases my hand.
I leave before I fall into him despite my new awareness.
I put Buddy back in his kennel and run to find Matt.
It's so dark.
Tombstone is still Tombstone.

It's a rough town where no girl should be out walking alone in the dark.

I run to one saloon after the other until I find them.

They're sitting at a patio table at the saloon behind the silver mine.

Ignoring that the patient is totally wasted, I turn to speak directly to Matt.

"Matt, you have to come to the motel. There has been a terrible accident and two of the guests have been hit by a car and killed. Craig is beside himself."

Matt looks shocked.

He sets down his glass and quickly dons his dress-coat and hat.

He looks at the patient and back at me.

"You go straight back there," he orders me. "I'll get James back safely. Tell Craig that I'll be there soon."

Matt gets up to pay the tab.

The patient sips his drink and doesn't look me in the eye.

"Lucky them," he mutters in his glass.

They've been talking.

The patient has been spilling his mind to poor Matt.

*There is no time to waste thinking about that.*

*If Craig sees the truth, so does Matt.*

*God, I have Angels around me!*

*Thank you.*

*If only James could see them too!*

I return to the motel and find Craig talking to the police.

I give him a nod to say that I found Matt and go back to my room.

I leave the door open.

The evening air is a welcoming blanket and I feel Craig watching out for me.

*No one will harm me.*

I lay on the bed in my clothes.

My mind is full of mixed thoughts and conflicting voices from my conscience.

*Just gather your things and leave.*
*Right now!*
*Wait for the patient to return and pass out,*
*take the keys and his wallet and run!*
*Take the laptop too!*
*All his passwords and banking and documents are on it.*
*You can stop along the way,*
*change the banking password,*
*buy time until you*
*can transfer funds to a new account.*
*There's at least one hundred thousand you can access right away!*
I once had access to all the banking information before we sold
James's business for one point two million dollars.
I was taken off signing rights once the monthly drafts started
clearing the bank.
He said it was to protect our investments from his previous wife,
that I wasn't to worry,
I just needed to ask.
Well that didn't transpire at all.
But I have my own money tucked away.
I have always had child support from the Children's dad.
I had also put myself on the payroll with the business and had
nothing to spend my money on.
When it sold, I had a little nest egg to spend on myself and
the Children.
I am happy that I have been frugal with it in case it be my only
money for a long time if he kills himself or I divorce him.
*You can swing this!*
*You would be okay for a little while!*
*Hire a mean lawyer.*
*You'll need a mean one when it comes to fighting for your freedom,*
*especially in regards to his soft spot:*
*money and control.*

*You can transfer everything right away and change his passwords.*
*You could call Wayne and tell him everything on the drive home,*
*or you could pack your things and go to Craig.*
*He will drive you to the airport when the patient is sleeping.*
*Craig will help!*
I'm almost asleep when the patient stumbles in.
He's standing over me,
still dressed in his gun slinger's costume.
He holds the prop pistol to my head.
"You better watch yourself, Colleen," he slurs. "You ever try and leave me you'll never see your ungrateful kids again."
I blink myself awake.
*What the fuck!*
My heart jumps as I realize what he is actually doing.
*He must feel vulnerable.*
*He knows that I could leave any second and he could not stop me.*
I don't know what else to do but laugh nervously at the black humour in his stumbling, drunken presence holding a prop gun to my head.
"What are you going to do?" I scoff. "Shoot me with your fake gun?"
He disgusts me.
I grab my pillow and blanket and move to the small couch on the other side of the room.
I don't want to breathe him in nor touch him in the slightest.
I feel weak and nauseous as the reality of his actions sink in.
*If the gun had been real,*
*would he have pulled the trigger?*
He stumbles around the bed,
takes off his overcoat,
and falls onto the covers.
The smell of whiskey and cigarettes permeates the room.
Alcohol is truth serum.

He has no inhibitions right now.
He might have given me the whole truth,
like a bullet in the head.
I decide to stay the course.
To flee would be my death penalty for loving him for far too long.
*I will know my window when it comes and I will never look back.*
*I will protect myself and my Children from any further damage.*
*I will get away soon.*
*Jayne's baby is coming and I will be gone soon.*
*Stay the course.*
I fall asleep.
I dream.
I dream of being in a hidden garden,
lulled by arms that love me,
slipping his hands beneath my skirt.

# CHAPTER 22

## The Call

*"For the first time in a long time I hear only my Self in my conscious thought, no longer accompanied by the reverb of a Higher Presence from whom I had been receiving answers. It feels strange.*
*As though I am totally on my own but not abandoned."*
– Colleen Songs

"You held a gun to my head, James," I whisper as he sleeps, watching him from across the room.

The clock on the bedside table shines six a.m.

The room is already warm.

Between the emotions of the evening before and not being
able to close my eyes after the patient's return to the motel, I'm
wide awake.

The reality and severity of his personality and his illness are glaring
after last night's events.

I had become complacent through years of attempts and many
threats, but no real action.

I console myself by going over all the people I asked to help,
all the counselling
workshops
and retreats.

*There's nothing we didn't encourage him to try!*

A gun to my head,
fake or not,
drunk or sober,
has really hit me.

The prayers I prayed as he drunkenly slumbered evaporated over
the bed.

Prayers for help,
prayers to my Children,
prayers to end this now,
for him to not even wake up.

I hear the whimper of the puppy and look over at his kennel.

He's waiting hopefully by the little gate to be let out and to
be loved.

*Just loved.*

*Me too, little fella.*

My thoughts are hollow.

For the first time in a long time I hear only my Self in my conscious thought, no longer accompanied by the reverb of a Higher Presence from whom I had been receiving answers.
It feels strange.
As though I am totally on my own but not abandoned.
I know the Higher Presence is still here, but its silence gives way to my own voice rising up.
I'm ready to be on my own and I'm very aware of what I'm dealing with.
The Higher Presence has released me of my training wheels.
I look over at the patient,
still deeply asleep.
I gently creep out of bed,
still dressed in my skirt and blouse.
I quickly brush my teeth and run a comb through my hair.
I pick up the leash and Buddy and we go outside.
It's quiet.
I head out toward the grassy area of the courtyard and let the puppy play in the blades of grass until he finds the right one to pee on.
I have to smile.
*My little guardian Angel, sorry I have been blind to you.*
His perfect little black face turns up to me.
I pick him up and cuddle him.
He wriggles in my arms to lick my neck and cheeks.
His puppy smell makes me melt into love.
"You only want to love and be received by those you love, don't you?" I say to him as I tuck my face into his soft puppy coat. "I promise I'll find you a place to be loved before I leave. You came on this trip for a reason too."
I hold him up so that we're looking at each other eye-to-eye.
"I'm going to find you a good home."
Walking back to the room, I see Craig talking to a couple of guests preparing to depart.

He looks over at me and I smile and blush a little bit.

No words are needed.

*He will always be that beautiful place I needed to visit to find my blush again.*

As I place the puppy back into his kennel, the patient stirs and reaches for his phone.

It's nine o'clock.

He looks like hell.

Puffy face,

pallid skin,

smelling of dirty smoke and stale alcohol.

I hold my breath and go to him to help him get out of bed.

*The sooner he gets cleaned up,*

*the sooner I can breathe again.*

He doesn't argue.

"I'm sorry," he mutters as I get him out of his garb from last night. I walk him to the bathroom.

"I'm so sorry," he says again before I can close the door.

"Just shower so we can go," I say impatiently. "You put a gun to my head last night. I just want to get going. We have to get back to Tucson to pick up the RV."

"I'm so sorry!" he repeats. "Colleen, I never meant to hurt you. All this. I'm sick, Colleen. I never meant to hurt you."

He's weeping.

I avoid touching him as he attempts to hold me through his weeping.

"Yes James, you are sick and you are drunk," I state as I hand him towels and run the water. "You are misunderstood and you are unloved. You are all those things that give you an excuse to continue to be an asshole. You put a bloody gun to my head last night!

"Just shower," utters my caregiver's voice. "You'll feel better after a long, hot shower. Then we'll eat and get back to Tucson. You need to settle down and get back into your routine."

I close the door and leave him to his own misery.

I busy myself with packing.

*We will go back to Tucson,*

*pick up the RV,*

*and find a place in Phoenix where he will be happy enough for me to leave.*

*He can take care of his own sorry ass after that.*

His cell rings.

My heart jumps.

I listen for the shower;

it's still running.

I answer his cell.

"Hello?" my voice cracks.

"Hey!" the voice of Jayne answers me. "Where are you?"

My heart feels like it's going to pound out of my chest.

"Tombstone," I whisper.

"Where is James?" she asks.

"In the shower," I whisper.

I'm quaking and excited and afraid all at once.

*I miss her.*

*Thank God for her.*

"I'm going to have the baby any day now," she hastily informs me.

"I sold my place. I'm living in a hospice till the baby comes and I'll need you in Oregon. I'm moving home. Let me call him in a few minutes. Hang up!"

I do as I'm told.

I fumble to erase the call from his phone.

The shower stops.

I put the phone down where he had left it.

I go back to the suitcases and continue packing.

I busy my trembling hands.

I hear the tap running as he brushes his teeth and I breathe a sigh of relief.

I take advantage of the extra moments to breathe deeper and become calmer.

*Jayne is having the baby soon!*
*Any day, she said!*
*Any day!*
He walks out of the bathroom naked.
I see an entirely different man than the one I fell in love with.
I have no attraction nor feeling for him at all.
I am free of him.
I hand him some clothes and decide to prepare some coffee to aid him in his waking.
His phone rings.
*FUCK I wish I had my own bloody phone!*
I recall the day we pulled away from our little house to begin this journey.
I was so distraught with grief.
I was out of body and out of mind.
He simply took my phone out of my hands.
I haven't seen it since.
*Only his stupid phone.*
*Such a fucking control freak!*
It rings again.
I see him look at it.
But rather than answer, he takes his sweet time dressing.
"Who could that be?" I ask him, trying to sound casual.
"It's Jayne," he says, putting on his second sock.
"Oh! You better answer," I exclaim in excitement. "She might be in labour."
He fastens his belt buckle and picks up the phone upon the final ring.
My heart falls back into place and I turn to the coffee maker to hide my angst.
He steps outside.
I can't hear his conversation.
*Fuck!*

*God, you REALLY try my patience!*
Even my body is salivating from the taste of my pending freedom.
I feel sweat trickling down my back.
I finish preparing the coffee,
pour him a cup,
and take it out to him.
I tug on his shirt to get his attention.
"So?" I whisper.
He smiles and continues talking.
I'm smiling too, genuinely happy about my friend's baby.
*I am going to owe you the rest of my days, Little One, whoever you are!*
He ends the call smiling.
"So?" I ask. "What's happening? Did she have the baby? Can I go
see her? I hope she wasn't alone."
"Not yet," he smiles and tries to shush all my questions with one
hand to my lips and the other around my waist.
I try not to cringe.
He pulls me over to stand in front of him and holds me close.
I feign a smile and look him in the eyes.
"She wants you to come to Oregon as she's moving back and
things are hectic," says the patient. "She is living in the hospice
right now as there are complications with the pregnancy and she
needs as much bed rest as possible. Her farm has been sold and
she has had help packing, but she can't leave Canada until the baby
is born. She will drive to Oregon as soon as she gets the okay and
she'll need help with finding a new place. She wants you there for
their American Thanksgiving dinner."
His eyes are happy.
He takes a sip of coffee.
"I was thinking though," he adds, "if we go to Yuma next, as soon
as possible, I can have some dental work done."
"Dental work?" I ask him, puzzled.
*Since when does he need dental work?*

"Matt told me about a great dentist last night after one of my fillings came out. The dentist can whiten my teeth and give me a check-up at the same time."

I tighten my stomach muscles as I notice his hands are still around my waist.

He must have felt the twinge because he removes his hold from my body.

"I don't remember many more details, but yeah," he stumbles on, "I have to get this filling fixed sooner rather than later."

He takes another sip of his coffee and then looks at me with sincerity.

"I was thinking," he says, "in the shower."

He pauses to breathe and looks down at his coffee cup.

"What is it?" I ask cautiously.

"Let's get settled in Yuma and you can go see Jayne and stay for a whole month. I know you miss your kids. Perhaps by seeing the baby you'll have your baby fix and you'll be ready to move on."

I can't believe my ears!

I can't believe his words!

My heart sinks into my guts.

His insanity is confirmed by his thoughts,

words,

and stupid idea that someone else's baby could replace my own.

*This man has NO IDEA what love is,*

*no idea what being a parent means!*

I shake my head.

"Perhaps," I sigh. "Let's get going then."

"But just so you know," his blue eyes shadow over as his voice takes on a warning tone, "I asked her to book a return flight to Phoenix as I'll need you after my treatments. Then we'll start our new life."

# CHAPTER 23

## The Knowing

*"…all I can see is dust, desert, and dirt.*
*Maybe it is just my mindset.*
*I can't see much beauty around me anymore."*
– Colleen Songs

*Yuma.*

*What is so bloody great about Yuma?*

I'm tired and still silent from the patient thinking I could EVER get over my Children by being with another's.

He's upset that his attempt at being "considerate" didn't steal my heart.

We said our goodbyes to our friends in Tombstone and drove back to Tucson to pick up the RV.

We picked up the Fifth Wheel and headed to Yuma.

I have heard so many stories about people heading to Yuma to retire.

Maybe it's great for them, but all I can see is dust, desert, and dirt.

Maybe it's just my mindset.

I don't see the beauty around me.

We drive in silence once again, not setting eyes on one another.

Buddy snuggles into my lap and once in a while whimpers for

a walk,

a kiss,

a cuddle.

I vow to find him a happy home before I leave.

The patient is silent as we find our way to the RV resort in Yuma.

The site promises good satellite reception, internet, and a gym: all the things the patient requires for any kind of contentment.

It's an over fifty-five gated resort and although the patient is only forty-six, they allow us in after he tells them he is retired and wants peace and quiet.

*Yes, retired at forty-six.*

*Life should be so much better than this hell.*

Driving through the town I'm annoyed with the heat.

There is dust on my skin and in my hair and teeth no matter where we go.

Seeing the dirt wisp around the truck windows, I become grumpier and grumpier;

tired,

annoyed,

and so ready to leave.

*I need water around me.*

*Water!*

*To wash away what's dead*

*and bring nourishment to my skin.*

*I cannot wait to get to Oregon,*

*to the ocean!*

We drive through the gate of the resort and tears fall down
my cheeks.

*Now this is nice!*

I know that this is it.

*This is the place!*

I know it.

I feel it.

*THIS is the place where I can leave him and not look back.*

*It couldn't be more perfect!*

The resort is groomed and lush with palm trees, flower boxes, wide
pathways, and large private sites where the patient can have his
space and let me be.

I'm amazed by the contrast of this resort and the desert outside
the perimeter.

*Two worlds colliding,*

*like the patient and me.*

One lush and full of life,

the other dusty,

hard,

and unforgiving.

*Years of trying to groom the desert.*

*That is our marriage.*

My heart constricts in my chest from the relief.

My freedom is just around the corner.

Tears continue to well in my eyes and I wipe them away.

*Not yet, Colleen.*

*Do not break down yet.*

*Be calm.*

*Be steady.*

*Take one day at a time.*

*You are almost there.*

I breathe in a slow, steady breath.

I look over at the patient.

He's looking at me as he slips the truck into park in front of the reception gate.

"It's so pretty here," I say with a forgiving smile for my thoughts about Yuma.

He smiles back and gets out of the truck to register us into the resort.

*Thank you, God!*

I open the channel to my Higher Power whether it's listening or not.

*This place is perfect.*

*I did not expect it to be, but I should have known it would be.*

*I am so grateful,*

*really I am!*

*I promise to settle your Child in nicely,*

*leave gracefully,*

*and let You take over.*

*I am so tired and this place is a blessing.*

Buddy stands up on my lap to look outside my window.

He whimpers and his tail begins to wag.

The patient comes out of the reception office and walks over to what looks like the ground's maintenance man.

They greet each other, talk briefly, then shake hands.

The patient walks back to the truck, gets in, and hands me some paperwork.

"Who was that?" I ask.

"A good carpenter," James replies happily. "I asked the receptionist if they knew of a good carpenter in the area and they said their maintenance man does a lot of work for the residents. She told me to go and ask him if he could do some work for us."

"Okay," I reply, somewhat surprised by this random, new need he has. "What work? When is he coming over?"

"Some things have been bugging me, like the closet and lack of shelving. If we're going to stay here a while, then I may as well get it done. He's giving us time to get settled in and then he'll be over tomorrow evening. He'll have his children with him as it will be after hours." James looks over at me cautiously. "I hope you don't mind."

I smile and look down at Buddy.

My heart warms from the instant understanding of this random circumstance.

I pet Buddy lovingly.

*You are going to meet your new family tomorrow, Buddy.*

"I don't mind," I say. "It's perfect."

*Absolutely perfect.*

# CHAPTER 24

## Black Morning

*"Everything will be better now,"* Mom reassures me.
*"Have some tea. You just needed a little clean-up."*
— Colleen Songs

The first morning in Yuma is met by the smell of coffee and toast. The usually welcome aroma isn't sitting well with me; its scent makes me nauseous.

As my feet hit the floor, my stomach takes a turn and I lunge myself to the bathroom.

I vomit blackened, slimy bile into the toilet.

Fever hits instantly as my body purges itself repeatedly.

The patient finds me clinging to the toilet.

My hands are clamped to the seat and cannot be pried off.

I convulse into spasms of pain and retching.

"What the hell, Colleen?" he shouts in a panic.

"I don't know. I don't know," I gasp between heaving.

The pain in my stomach is excruciating and begins to take over my every limb.

The patient finds a cloth and runs it under cold water for me.

*Why is my vomit black?*

The patient returns and places the cloth on my neck.

I'm now his patient.

"Oh God, Colleen! What have I done to you?" he asks, scrambling to find a way to help me.

I'm confused about why, where, and how this is happening.

"Why is this your problem?" I heave one more time.

*I don't want to die before I get home!*

"What. Are you. Talking. About?" I sink to the floor, grateful for the closeness of the wall and toilet holding me into a hurl position with no effort on my part.

"All this! All this!" he flusters.

I shake my head and wave my hand at him.

*I really cannot take your self-blaming right now.*

*It does not work anymore.*

"Go away," I choke, with an impulse to vomit again. "Just go. Make tea."

My Mother's remedy for everything.

*Mom!*

Tea.

Hot.

Sweet.

Hydrating.

I don't know how long I sit there, wedged between the toilet and the wall, but the niche's coolness is comforting.

As the vomiting subsides my heart slowly finds a smoother pace.

I remove the cloth from my neck and wipe my face.

I allow myself time to recover.

*What the hell is wrong with me?*

I try and make my way to the sofa bed.

I notice that I have soiled myself and I begin to cry.

I stumble into the shower and shed my clothes.

The stench is overwhelming and I vomit again.

The patient returns with my tea and places it on the vanity counter.

"Oh God, Colleen!"

He turns on the shower and begins to wash me.

I reach for my shower gel, anything to rid the smell that keeps turning my stomach.

I push his hands away.

"Don't touch me," I beg. "Please don't touch me."

I am crying again and each sob sends rancid fluid purging from my body.

The diarrhea is terrible and embarrassing and it feels like acid on my skin.

I pray the water will send the blackness away,

far,

far away from me.

"I need to get away from it all," I mumble.

I'm dizzy and I can't stop crying.

Pain swims and dives around every cell of my body.

I almost welcome the fire it creates,

cauterizing open wounds deep inside me,

so deep;

years of wounds.

I reach for the portable showerhead as my stomach settles into a
folding ache.

I hold the spray to my chest.

Water runs down my stomach,

down,

down to the drain.

"God!" I mumble. "Oh God, I'm tired. I'm so very, very tired."

I rest my head against the shower wall and fall asleep.

I hear the faint sound of someone close by.

I look through the shower doors and see the patient crouched
down with his forehead against the glass, eyes closed as though
in prayer.

I look away and close my eyes.

I just close my eyes.

*I just need a few moments.*

I begin to dream.

I dream of warm laughter and the warm scent of my Mom's
Finnish sweet bread baking in the oven.

Cinnamon.

Cardamom.

I dream I'm sharing lunch with my Children around a table.

I dream of a little house where they come in with their friends and
fill the rooms.

I dream.

Hands are cleaning the insides of my heart.

I dream.

Light is cleaning the inside caverns of my organs to get ready for
a party.

I dream.

It's a party for me!

The Children are here!
They are toddlers from the time before I met James.
I see them.
I hear them.
I dream.
I'm floating.
My Mother is here.
She's having tea and playing games at the table with my Children.
I join them.
I feel clean and fresh and we're having a lovely time.
"Feeling better, my Lovey?" Her voice rings through my dream.
"Yes, Mom. I feel a lot better."
I sit,
pick up my Children,
and place them on my knee.
Like that day in the doctor's office so many years before.
I feel their warmth.
I feel their pudgy softness.
I hear their giggles and chatter with their Mummu.
"Everything will be better now," Mom reassures me. "You just
needed a little clean-up. Have some tea."
I feel my heart well up with so many emotions:
missing emotions,
grieving emotions,
loving emotions,
regretting emotions,
longing emotions.
"Mom!" I cry.
"What?" a voice asks me.
"Oh Mom!" I ache for her words.
"Hey, wake up, Colleen," says a voice that isn't my Mother's.
Confused emotions.
'Where am I?' emotions.

I awaken.

I'm in bed,

not the sofa bed.

I'm in the bedroom.

I'm in his bed.

"Wake up, Colleen."

It's the patient's voice.

My eyes focus on him.

Then I remember the floating.

*He must have carried me to bed.*

I cringe.

*He touched me.*

*He has seen my body.*

*He had to touch my bare skin to put me into bed.*

"Are you okay?" he asks, kneeling beside the bed.

"Yeah, I think so." I pull myself up to sit against the pillows.

I pull the blankets tightly around my body.

I notice that I feel no pain.

"Just lay quiet. I have some tea for you."

He hands me a warm cup of tea.

I take it and the aroma brings me back to my dream.

I tear up.

"I'm sorry!" he implores me.

"I don't understand," I say. "Sorry for what?"

I'm puzzled.

"Did you poison me or something?" I ask him.

Terror creeps in.

"Why didn't you bring me to the hospital?" I freak out.

I am too weak to jump out of bed.

*I've got to get to the hospital!*

"I've asked for too much from you," he says, resting his head in his

hands, blocking me from swinging my legs over in an attempt to get up and go find a doctor. "All I've done to you. All of this has made you sick. All of this has hurt you so much."

"What the fuck, James! Why didn't you bring me to the hospital?"
I feel my head start to ache.

"You must have just caught a bug in Tombstone or something," he replies. "I was watching you. I used to be in rescue, remember? I don't blame you for not believing in me anymore, for not believing I can take care of you. It must have been the long days and the miles of travelling and the stress I've put you through."
I have no words for him.

My heart slows its pace at the reality that I wasn't poisoned;
that he is just making this about himself,
as usual.
*I probably just had a bug but it sure hit fast.*
I'm done with words.
I sit back and try to relax again,
breathing away the fright and overwhelming anger.
I begin to remember my dream,
and as my breathing calms my body and mind,
I feel in my heart that my body is simply purging.
*Mom said I needed a little clean-up.*
*I am finally in a place where I can somewhat let go of all his poison.*
*He's been poisoning me for years.*
My body has always been in tune with my emotional state.
This makes sense to me.

"I need some quiet time in one place," I dismiss him as I sip my tea, "and so do you. You will have some time here to settle down and I will have some time with Jayne in Oregon."

"I don't think you should go anywhere," he says, his brow furrowed with concern. "You should get help in Phoenix with me when I go."

He avoids looking me in the eye.

"Help for what?" I say. "I need rest. YOU need help."

*You sure like to pounce on me when I am weak,*
*but you are not stopping me.*
*Not this time.*
*I made a deal with God!*
"You need help to get over your children," he blurts out with
venom. "I've been thinking about how sick this is making you and
I get so angry at them."
He puts his head back in his hands.
I breathe,
trying to keep calm.
*Just breathe.*
*But, God!*
*You are really pissing me off!*
*I cannot take any more of this craziness.*
*I just shit myself while vomiting and passed out in the shower and I have to deal*
*with Your brat now?*
*Jesus!*
*I have had enough!*
I breathe.
There's no arguing with the patient about my Children and I won't
feed his implications.
He doesn't deserve my Children.
*He is never going to stop.*
*He will always blame someone else for his hateful behaviour.*
I sit myself up further on the pillows and I'm surprised that I
feel fine.
I feel a bit of muscle pain from all the vomiting,
but I'm otherwise fine,
recharged,
rested
and fine.
"Look, James," I say firmly, "I need to go see my friend who will
be having a new baby BY HERSELF. My friend who is moving

back to Oregon BY HERSELF. My friend who has helped us out many times. I'm not going to argue about this. It's set."

*He's not going to get me to go anywhere else with him except to the airport!*

"My time away perfectly coincides with your appointments in Phoenix," I continue. "When I'm back we'll see how you are. YOU need this time for yourself to relax, to focus on yourself, to do what you need to do. I'll use this time to get out of your way and help my friend."

A thought hits me that might flip his thinking.

"Look, you're right! Look at how you took care of me just now. I'm thankful for your kindness. Now let me do the same for you and for our good friend." I smile and nod my head. "Okay?"

He turns to look at me.

His jaw tightens and his blue eyes scan my face to see any signs of a nefarious plan to leave him.

I hold a good poker face.

Then he softens.

"Okay, Colleen," he says. "You're right. Okay. Your being sick scared me."

He sinks deeper onto my side of the bed and kneels down, elbows supporting his weight.

"I just don't want to share you with anyone. I don't know what I'd do if I lost you, but I know I have to get better. Do you understand?"

*No one can be normal and think the way he does.*

*He is so sick.*

"It's fine, James. I'm only going to see Jayne."

I feel my throat tightening at the slightest thought of any further delay in escaping this life with him.

*I have GOT to get out of here.*

"I'm exhausted," I say, attempting to change the subject. "That must have been some bug. Did I leave you a horrible mess?"

He shakes his head and reassures me that he cleaned it all up and
that it wasn't that bad.

He did the laundry as I slept.

The patient reaches for my hand and folds it in both of his.

My skin crawls.

I pray to strike away any idea of what he might have done to me
when he put me to bed after I passed out.

I hope I was such a stinky mess that he didn't do anything.

I laugh inside at my own suspicious thoughts and their irony.

*He doesn't touch me when I'm all dressed up;*

*he certainly wouldn't when I'm full of shit and vomit.*

"You're so beautiful," he says, leaning in to caress my hand with
his lips.

"I have been all along, James. I need rest," I say, and ease my hand
away from his.

I wrap my hands around my teacup.

I take a sip of my tea to dismiss him.

He stands up and leaves the room.

I hear the door open and his footsteps outside of the RV.

I hear the faint flick of his lighter through the open window.

I don't know what made me so sick, but I choose to think it was my
Mom's energy visiting me, purging me of the imprints of his abuse.

*It is time to be quiet.*

*Sit still.*

*Get him into a routine.*

*Get ready to go see Jayne.*

*You are going if it kills you.*

*You are going.*

## CHAPTER 25

## Fuck Off

"*I'm not mad.*
*I'm just done talking to him.*
*I'm done hearing his voice.*
*It's all I have left to say.*
*Fuck off.*
*I turn back to the kitchen and prepare myself some soup.*"
– Colleen Songs

*I must have fallen back to sleep.*
I hear children.
I roll over to check the time on my watch that I keep on the
window sill beside me.
*Seven o'clock.*
I stretch and my stomach is a little sore but otherwise I feel fine.
The bed feels good.
*I forgot how good this bed felt.*
*Damn him!*
I hear the sound of children laughing again.
*Why am I hearing children?*
I sit for a few moments on the side of my bed and allow the sounds
to surround me.
*Oh yes.*
I recall the carpenter and his children were coming over.
I listen to their lilting voices.
*A little boy and a little girl*, I guess to myself.
*He's the older one.*
I hear the sound of puppy growls and children's laughter.
They're beautiful sounds.
*Sissy!*
*Andrew!*
*What are you doing right now?*
*What are you feeling right now?*
I feel the warmth of my love for them well up in my chest.
I feel their power fill me up starting at my toes,
flooding into my legs,
warming my belly where I nurtured them to life,
and then surging to my arms and fingers.
It gives me resolve and I quickly freshen up and dress.
I see myself in the mirror and notice that I'm glowing.
My skin is pink and clean.
*Keeping your word, Universe?*

*Thank you, Mom!*

I step out of the Fifth Wheel and see the patient talking to the maintenance man, who is wrapped in a carpenter's belt.

"Hi," I greet him.

A very tall, dark, handsome man extends his huge hands to take mine and smiles the friendliest smile.

"Nice to meet you," he says to me, his rich Spanish accent filling my ears.

"You're awake now," says the patient, looking relieved and smiling politely. "I didn't want to disturb you, but now that you're awake, we can get that closet work done. Peter has time now if we don't mind his children waiting here."

The patient turns his attention back to the carpenter.

"If you want to start on the shelving in the closet, now would be perfect timing."

Both the patient and Peter walk into the RV and begin assessing what needs to be done.

The closet by the front entrance is pretty useless.

We don't use it other than for stuffing things we don't want into it and quickly slamming the door.

But one good bump in the road knocks the closet door open and scatters the contents all over the floor.

Peter's job would be to build shelves with three-inch lips on the front to hold everything in place.

While Peter and the patient talk shelves, I sit down at the picnic table and slowly breathe in the warm afternoon fragrances.

Flowers grow along each RV site.

A sandy,

earthy,

sweet fragrance

swarms around my nostrils.

This is a much better impression than the one I had when I first arrived here.

*This is how I want to remember Yuma.*

Everywhere I go in my life I discover a new scent.

Each new scent is connected to a memory of a song, a person, a moment, or an experience.

Feelings of love, joy, pain, happiness;

events of births, deaths, meetings, weddings, travel.

The depths of sadness and longing are the fragrances I've collected over time.

I close my eyes and evoke the scent of my Daughter.

*Mmmmm, yes.*

*My gorgeous little tomboy.*

*Leather,*

*soil,*

*carnations.*

My Son.

I giggle.

He smelled of my Dad's Old Spice,

right from the moment of birth.

'Little Frank' we'd call him, after my Dad.

*Nutmeg,*

*citrus,*

*gasoline.*

I open my eyes.

I look around for the carpenter's children and spot them sitting inside the dog kennel staring at me.

Buddy is quietly nestled on the little girl's lap and her older brother is standing at the side of the kennel, closest to me.

I smile and take them all in.

I look at Buddy,

blissful and content.

I can feel his calm heart.

*Hey, little guy.*

*You found your family.*

"Hi," I greet the children.

The little girl puts her finger up to her mouth.

"Shh," she says quietly. "I just got him sleeping."

"Do you love this puppy?" a gruff voice asks me.

The deep voice of the boy surprises me.

"How old are you two?" I ask.

"Five," whispers the girl.

"Seven," gruffs the boy.

I chuckle and walk over to them.

I sit beside the kennel.

"He's a pretty cute pup, isn't he?" I ask. "He sure likes you.'

The boy looks over his shoulder at his sister.

I watch his eyes.

They are full of admiration and love.

*He adores his little sister.*

"She likes how soft he is," he says affectionately.

We sit and watch Buddy whimper away on the little girl's lap.

In the background, their father is cutting and hammering.

The little girl narrows her eyes,

annoyed her Dad is working when the dog is sleeping.

Sure enough, Buddy stirs, scrambling up to her face for
more kisses.

She giggles and cries out to her father, "Daddy! You woke
the puppy."

Her brother sits down beside her.

Buddy leaps into his arms and licks his face and neck.

Both children laugh, smothered in love.

I go into the Fifth Wheel to get four popsicles.

"I think Buddy found his family," I whisper in the patient's ear as I
pass him.

He looks over to them and nods.

I sit back down beside the kennel and hand each child a popsicle,
distracting Buddy with one of his own.

He laps away on it as ferociously as a puppy can.

The children laugh and slurp and giggle as they watch him eat his icy treat through the slats of the kennel.

It's a moment of pure love.

*Thank you for this Band Aid, Universe.*

*I needed this to keep me going,*

*going home.*

The carpenter finishes the patient's project within an hour.

He hands Peter the promised cash but the big friendly giant shakes his head.

"I wonder," he asks politely, "I wonder if that pup is for sale. We've been thinking about getting them a puppy but I wasn't sure until now how they would be with one."

He smiles.

The patient looks at me and shrugs but says nothing.

We all look over at the kids and smile.

"Hey, guys," I implore, bargaining with the kids. "Do you think you could take good care of Buddy? Would he be a good trade for your Dad's work?"

*The patient appears to actually like children.*

He gives the little guy a high-five to seal the deal and laughs.

I feel a pinch in my heart.

*You used to be that nice to my Children,*

*only on your terms,*

*only when YOU felt good,*

*only when it pleased you.*

*When times got tough, you tossed us.*

*GAH!!!*

I close my eyes to shut him out.

*He does not deserve my grieving over what once was.*

*He does not deserve any further emotion from me.*

"Alrighty then," I say, diving into the excitement of the children and their new dog.

I gather all of Buddy's things:
his bed and kennel,
his little harness and leash,
his food and bowls,
his treats and toys.
*Thank you, Universe.*
*Thank you for coming through on your word.*
*Just a few more things to prepare and I can go too.*
*Thank you.*
I smile through my tears.
"Awe, you're crying!" pouts the little girl.
"Oh, I'm so very happy puppy found a family," I say. "What will
you name him? He's still young enough for you to give him a name
of your own."
I kneel down to the children's eye level as they struggle to hold
Buddy's wiggling body in their arms.
"Licorice!" they both shout in unison.
"Licorice?" I laugh.
"Yeah," screeches the boy. "He's black and he likes to lick us."
"That's perfect!"
They pack their new bundle into the truck and head home.
I feel a little bit empty despite knowing it's for the best.
He did keep the energy a bit lighter in our lives.
The air is beginning to cool and I go into the RV looking for food.
The patient follows me in.
"How are you feeling?" he asks.
I am uncertain as to whether he's talking about how I feel about
the puppy
or if he's asking about how I am personally feeling.
*He actually sounds like he cares.*
I don't want to argue
or debate
or feel anything

other than the love those children have for that wee puppy,
so I remain neutral in my response.
"Just hungry," I say, while searching the kitchen cupboards.
"Maybe I'll have some soup."
"You don't mind giving up the puppy?"
I stop what I'm doing and look at him.
"James," I breathe, "you need to focus with no distractions."
*That is all I am going to say.*
"Colleen," he reaches out and takes my hands.
I stand still.
"I gave you that puppy," he pouts, his mouth a frown.
I breathe.
My body tightens from his touch.
*Quit touching me already!*
"I'm sorry I've let you down so many times," he continues. "I
thought the puppy would help you. I didn't think you'd just
give him away like that. But I'm seeing how easy it is for you to
give up."
He lets my hands go and tucks his into his pockets.
He sways back and forth on his heels.
"You gave me that puppy to replace my own Children," I say. "Can
you not see how crazy that is? No. You CAN'T see. It was nice
to see these children happy and it made me happy to give them
something you don't even understand. So. Just. Fuck. Off."
I'm not angry.
I'm simply done talking to him,
done hearing his voice.
*Fuck off.*
*That's all I have left to say.*
I turn back to the kitchen and prepare myself some soup.

# CHAPTER 26

## Packing

———

*"If I was still in love with him,*
*if I knew he had ever really loved me,*
*the grief of leaving him would consume me...*
*Instead, I am consumed by the grief of lost time."*
— Colleen Songs

The RV is quiet:
no whimpering puppy,
no playing with toys,
no begging for treats.
There's no crate to trip over,
no bowl of water to step in.
I vacuum and clean his scent away to keep from being reminded of
what he symbolized:
replacing my Children.
*God I'm so fed up!*
I smile at the memory of the children who attached their hearts to
him a couple of days earlier.
I pray little Licorice is loved beyond measure.
The days drift by.
If I was still in love with the patient,
if I knew he had ever really loved me in the past,
the grief of leaving him would consume me.
When I love,
I love deeply.
Instead, I'm consumed by the grief of lost time,
the lies he told,
the time I've missed with my Children,
the pain they were too young to experience but did anyway.
Though I'm sodden with this regretful grief for my little family,
there's a sense of calm and peace around me like a buffer.
I pace myself as I prepare for my journey home.
I make lists of things to prepare.
I putter with cleaning and laundry.
I sing to myself to avoid making conversation that may lead
to confrontation.
I pray to my Children and talk to them in silent pleasure.
I'm ready for the journey to begin my new life.
I'm stronger and wiser,

full with Me,
full with my Children,
full with knowing we gave it all we could,
full with what we have now and who we grew into,
free to build a life that is all ours,
guarded within my fortress.
I'm resolved of my debt.
I've paid in full plus interest.
It's more than enough.
It's all we need and want.
I'm in a rhythm.
I smile.
*We're going to live in three-quarter time for a long time, Children.*
*Just the three of us waltzing through a better life.*
He's in a routine.
Between heart beats we find our way around one another.
I repeat positive affirmations to keep my timing steadily
moving forward.
It is like God has placed a blanket around each of us.
Even the air seems calmer.
*It is pleasant enough.*
*It does not have to be more.*
*He came to me when I needed him.*
*I was there for him when he needed me.*
*Right?*
Thoughts and memories come and go like air.
Today is a day of sorting clothes and packing what I need for my
'quick trip'.
I cannot let him see that I will not be returning.
*I cannot pack everything.*
*I have to let some things go.*
I pack one thing at a time.
*One carry-on,*

*one little duffle bag.*
*I can do laundry at Jayne's.*

She called last night when I was cleaning the kitchen after supper,
drying each plate and re-arranging the cupboards, thinking of the
list I'd have to make to stock the fridge and shelves for the patient
when it was time for me to go.
I'd have to prepare enough food to last him at least a few days.
I'd have to make a point of talking to him about it,
asking him what he'd like,
asking him what he wants me to prepare in advance.
While going through my mental checklist the phone rang.
"Hey, Jayne," answered the patient from his rocker.
He had been watching the news before he was interrupted.
I went about my tasks with my ears perked and my breath slow.
"That's great!" he said. "I'll let her know. She's been preparing
already so I won't go hungry while she's gone."
He laughed at something Jayne told him and then passed the
phone to me.
"Hey, Jayne!" I welcomed her voice and told myself to focus on
staying girlish and light during the conversation, *like this is just one of*
*those quick 'girl-time' trips.*
"I'm not bringing much," I told her in response to her question
about how much I'll be bringing. "I'll take a couple changes of
clothes and rain gear and hikers. I know you'll be putting me to
work, and its rainy there in November."
We laughed, said our goodbyes, and then I gave the cell back to
the patient.
"Jayne wants to give you the flight details," I said in answer to his
questioning look.
He reached for the cell and continued the conversation, making
notes in his agenda.
"Tomorrow night. 7:10 departure?" he hesitated.

My heart skipped a beat but I went on about my tasks.

"Okay, I'll have her there by five. Thanks. And you have my credit card number for her return flight?" His head nodded and he smiled.

He said goodbye and his rocking resumed.

The Fifth Wheel was silent except for the incessant wheezing from the back and forth of his chair.

Nothing else.

"I'm so glad I've been getting things ready," I cheer and continue to flutter about with my checklist. "All your favourite foods and snacks are ready. You'll have enough to do you for a few days. Tomorrow I'll do laundry and pack. Everything will be ready so that you'll have nothing to worry about during your appointments in Phoenix."

He rocked in silence.

I put the kettle on to make us some chamomile tea.

As I prepared it, he turned off the TV with the remote.

Still silent.

Still rocking.

I set his steaming cup of tea beside him and placed mine on the dining table.

He took my hand.

I gave him a smile instead of the grimace I felt coming over my face.

"I'm so excited to see the new baby!" I said...

It's four in the afternoon,

two hours before I have to be at the airport.

I want to allow just enough time for him to drop me off and go.

No hanging around.

No minutes wasted arguing.

No time for anything to happen to keep me from getting on that flight.

As I zip up the duffle bag, I look around to be sure I don't leave behind anything I need, and that I leave what needs to be left as a ruse that I'll be returning to him.

My first-year anniversary present from him, a white and yellow gold bracelet, is still tucked into the drawer beside his matching, more masculine one.

*Check.*

*He wouldn't think I'd leave that behind.*

I bought them both, I recall.

*I never used to take it off.*

My book of songs is still tucked onto my bookshelf above my headboard.

I grab it and stuff it into my bag.

*Check.*

I remember the picture of my Children hidden in my drawer.

I listen for him.

He's outside smoking.

It's clear.

I quietly open the drawer and find the small silver folding picture frame holding both my Children, protecting them.

I slip it into the centre of my carry-on and zip everything up.

*Snug as a bug.*

*Check.*

Two pairs of jeans,

two t-shirts,

two sweaters,

four sets of 'under things',

four pairs of socks,

runners,

hikers,

rain suit,

bathing suit for the hot-springs we always go to when I visit her,

wind vest,

one pair of running pants,
one sports bra, and
my toiletries.
*Check.*
I see my guitar case sitting sweetly at the foot of the bed.
I'm taken back to last night,
last night when he proved,
once again,
why I need to get away from him forever.


I set his steaming cup of tea beside him and placed mine on the
dining table.
He took my hand.
I gave him a smile instead of the grimace I felt coming over
my face.
"I'm so excited to see the new baby!" I said.
He stood up from his rocking chair and led me to the bedroom.
He held me in his arms.
My body stiffened as I tried to receive the repulsive physical
contact as a casual hug.
"You'll be okay," I said, reassuring him with a firm and friendly pat
on the back.
Inside I was trembling,
uncertain as to what to do,
uncertain as to why he was suddenly feeling all mushy.
*A little too late.*
Uncertain as to his intentions, afraid he wouldn't let me go alive if
I fight him I try to relax within his hold.
For a moment the warmth of him reminded me of how long it had
been since I've been held.
I couldn't read his body language other than it was oddly silent
and demanding.
He released me from his hold only to grab my shoulders.

He held onto me so tightly that it pinched.

He hurt me but I showed no fear.

"What is it?" I asked.

I refused to struggle so as not to feed the thoughts in his mind that I could not read.

*Do not panic.*

*Be calm.*

"Promise me you'll not call your children?" he said, his grip tightening a little, shaking me just enough to emphasize his demands. "Promise me you'll come back? I'm doing this out of good faith. We still have a chance. I'll get better. We can start new. You and me."

It was as though he wasn't talking to me at all.

It was distant.

Over me.

Like he was talking to himself

or that other voice in his head that screwed with his reasoning.

He pulled me right into him and wrapped his arms around me.

My hands hung by my side.

I realized that this was the last time he would hold me.

I realized I was almost truly free.

I saw a door in front of me open.

I mentally slipped though it and closed it behind me.

I felt bathed in light with my wings wide open,

ready to take flight.

His hands began to tour my body.

My skin began to crawl.

*That's right!*

*I no longer belong to you.*

*I am mine.*

"Let's just focus on you getting well right now," I stepped back and wriggled out of his grip. "Jayne won't let me call the kids; she's on your side. You've made that very clear."

It was a lie.

"Don't worry," I added, "I get it. As for us, let's please take it slow. After everything we've talked about and your need to get better I have lots of things to sort out and you have to focus on getting well."

I touched his shoulders for reassurance.

As I turned to leave he grabbed me again and held me to his chest.

"I don't want this right now," I told him calmly. "I'm having my tea and then going to bed. Let me go."

He pushed me on the bed.

His expression was that of distaste,

the mocking smirk of a sore loser.

I hit the end of the mattress and slid off,

falling on top of my guitar case.

Her stifled strings cried out to ask if I was okay.

The impact gave voice to the years of rejection I've stifled inside my gut of denial.

I sat there stunned and embarrassed.

My throat tightened as tears pooled from the shock of the fall.

"You were never that attractive to me anyway!" he spewed in my face.

He walked out of the room,

out of the RV,

his footsteps fading into the distance.

# CHAPTER 27

## Do Not Look Back

*"I remember all of this and in turn,
my last lie to him
pales in comparison.
"See you soon," I say."*
— Colleen Songs

I decide to bring my beloved guitar with me just in case I want to write a song for Jayne's new baby.

That's the best excuse I can come up with to quench his suspicious eyes as I place it in the truck with my carry-on.

*I need her.*

*If it means handing her back to him at the airport she will understand.*

*If it risks him destroying her after he finds out I am not returning, she will forgive me.*

*But I need to try to bring her along.*

I go through my mental checklist again.

As my last task, I make sure to confirm all of the patient's appointments and prepay his fees over the phone.

*He loves money more than people.*

*If his treatment is already paid for, then he will not waste the money.*

*He will go for sure.*

*He needs to go.*

*I doubt he actually will go,*

*but that's not up to me to encourage any longer.*

*He needs to get well for himself.*

Satisfied that I've remembered everything, I climb into the passenger seat of the truck and await him as he closes and locks the RV.

I glance at the Fifth Wheel through my rear-view mirror.

*I hope I never see you again.*

*You have been my prison.*

*But I hope you find joy within your walls one day.*

I turn my attention to the windshield.

*I will only look forward.*

I buckle up as the patient gets behind the wheel.

He's silent.

I expect him to start his usual demands and threats about the Children, but he remains silent as we drive through Yuma to the airport.

*Goodbye, Yuma.*

*I never want to return to you.*
We drive as the sun reaches the horizon.
*Soon it will set.*
*How fitting, Jayne.*
*Thank you,*
*my friend,*
*for this timing.*
Red-gold sweeping colours are beginning to fill the sky.
We drive.
The parking lot is full of vehicles but we find a spot and park.
He gathers my bags.
I wrap my purse strap across my chest so that both my hands can
hold on to my freedom.
One hand holds my ticket and passport,
the other hand holds my guitar.
I ask the clerk at the check-in counter if I can take my guitar as
my carry-on.
She says the flight is full and I would have to check it.
I can't bear the thought of my precious guitar being tossed
or damaged.
The patient reaches to take her from my grip.
I can't look at her.
I manage a smile but I'm beginning to crumble as I feel her slip
from my fingers.
"It'll be with me when you get back," the patient says softly.
I hear her voice strumming in my ear,
in my heart.
"I'll be okay," she sings. "I'll come back to you."
I brush the fear away and trust her as I always have.
I secure my ticket and passport again in my right hand as my left
hand finds my purse.
We stop at a small convenience store to buy ChapStick and gum
for the flight.

The patient takes the bag of items from the clerk before I can.
He looks annoyed and edgy.
He stays quiet but his body language begins its edgy twitch and
restless stance.
We walk to the security gate.
I'm also getting restless.
I'm nervous that at any moment something will snap in him.
I hand my ticket and passport over to the security guard.
He takes his time reviewing these items.
*Oh God!*
*Enough already!*
*My nerves are shredding!*
I smile and cheerfully chat to him about going to see my best
friend who's having her first baby.
*Her Baby.*
*My Guardian Angel.*
The security guard hands me my ticket and passport and waves
me through.
Time stands still.
Everything moves slowly.
I'm encased in jello.
The air is thick and gravity pulls heavily at my limbs.
I can feel my heart beat.
I can hear the blood pump from my head,
through my heart,
to my toes
traveling back to the space between my eyes.
I look at my patient.
He stands beside me,
holding my guitar.
I see the image of the man I once loved.
But it's only an outline,
an empty guitar case.

Chords no longer connect our hearts.
A melody no longer sings our song.
James is gone.
I'm already on a new page.
My hearing is foggy.
My heart is constricting.
*This is death:*
*death of empty promises,*
*death of an empty marriage,*
*death of a part of my past that I know I need to forgive in order to forget.*
The departures hallway is the portal to my new life.
Memories flash before my eyes like I'm dying.
I see flashes of him in the doctor's office.
I see flashes of him when he first met my Children.
I see my Daughter running to the couch to jump between us when
we watched the lightning storm on the deck.
I see my Son playing catch with James on the front lawn.
I see James waiting for me at the end of the aisle on our
wedding day.
As I walked towards him, each step was blind to his lies.
Lies that wash the good memories away and uncovered the real
James, the patient.
I see the faces of the women who replaced me.
I remember every fun moment turning to pain if it wasn't
about him.
I remember nights of tearful rejection after being denied a simple
kiss goodnight.
I remember my Son curled up in his bed hurting from words he
never deserved.
I remember the patient's arms gripping my Daughter.
Let her go!
Let her go!
I remember his words.

The name-calling,
cutting,
and accusing,
while he broke vow after vow.
I remember all of this and in turn,
my last lie to him
pales in comparison.
"See you soon," I say.
He nods and slides his free arm around my waist to hug me.
He leans in for a kiss and I offer my cheek.
I push away from him and begin walking down the hallway to
my gate.
My back is still warm from his hand.
I mentally freeze the spot and throw the imprint of it away,
off of my body.
I don't look back.
*He will know I am not returning if I do not look back.*
*He will know without my telling.*
I do not look back.
I do not look back.
I do not look back.

# CHAPTER 28

## Sunset on the Wingtip

*"You cannot breathe life into someone refusing to inhale."*
– Colleen Songs

I do not look back.

I find my gate.

I do not look back.

I find an empty chair in the passenger waiting area.

I do not look back.

I sit.

I do not look back though I know by now I am out of his sight.

I place my carry-on in front of me,

between my legs.

I set my purse on top of my carry-on and tie the strap to
the handle.

I'm sweating.

Beads of sweat pour off my face and splatter on my lap.

I begin to tremble.

A hot burning flame releases from my belly.

I cry.

Aloud I cry.

I grab my stomach to brace the sobs that are coming from the
depths of my soul.

I can't control it.

The crowd around me fades.

I cry.

I ache.

I collapse against my bags.

I simply cry,

cry,

and cry,

and cry.

I feel arms around me and the scent of lilac fills my nostrils.

I don't care who it is.

I need to be held.

"Sweet Jesus hold me!" my voice begs the receiver of anyone listening. "Please just hold me!"

"There, there," says a woman's tender voice.

Her arms hold me gently but tightly.

I hear the jangle of silver and gold bracelets against her soft skin.

I cry.

She takes me closer into her arms.

She lets my head rest against her ample bosom.

I submit to the comfort and I cry.

Other hands take my ticket from mine.

I'm cradled for a few more sweet moments.

"Baby, it's time for my flight," says the lilac woman. "I have to go, sweet baby."

She takes my face in her hands and wipes the tears from my eyes with her thumbs.

She kisses my forehead.

"There, there. You'll be all right now."

I open my eyes to the friendly loving faces of a beautiful ebony woman who held me and the striking man who took my ticket.

He hands me back my ticket and offers me a tissue from his pocket.

"Your flight is coming soon," he says in a deeply soothing drawl.

"Don't you worry now. You'll be okay. I just know it."

The woman kisses my forehead one more time.

Then the pair smile,

take each other's hand,

and walk away.

I gather my bags and go to the ladies' room.

I look into the mirror:

eyes swollen,

makeup smeared down my cheeks.

"You've never been more beautiful than you are right now," I tell her.

I splash my face with cool water and comb my hair.

Exhausted,

aching,

relieved

I walk back toward my gate to wait for my flight.

I find a payphone and dial Mae's number.

One ring.

Two rings.

My call is answered and received after the operator's request to accept the charges.

"Well, hello!" rings Mae's voice.

"Mae," I whisper. "Mae, why am I crying?"

She chuckles.

"I don't know. Why are you crying?"

"I'm leaving him now," I sputter. "I'm at the airport in Yuma and I'm finally leaving him. Why am I crying?"

I start crying again, holding her voice to my ear to absorb anything, everything she can offer me.

"He doesn't deserve my tears," I cry.

Mae lets me give into my emotions for a few more moments.

"No, but you do," she soothes. "You do. You gave two hundred and fifty percent to that man. You deserve those tears. You did it!. He has to find his own way now. You've proven that no matter how much you loved that man or tried to help him, it was never enough."

*It is true.*

*You cannot breathe life into someone refusing to inhale.*

*Well, I am going to inhale!*

*Inhale ME!*

*My Children!*

*My Mother!*

*My Father!*

*My Family!*

*My Life!*

*My Self!*

*Me!*

I smile through my tears and wipe the last traces of them from my face.

"I'm finally coming home," I laugh.

"Yes," she laughs with me. "You're coming home. And your Children are going to be okay. YOU are going to be okay."

"Yaaay!" I chime.

"Yaaay!" she chimes.

I hear my flight being announced.

"I'm catching my flight now. I have to go so I can come home."

"Okay. Get on that flight. I love you."

"Love you too, Mae. Thank you."

I collect my bags and head to my gate.

I smile as I feel my Children getting closer with every step.

I board the plane and find my seat by the window.

I buckle my seatbelt

and as the plane coasts down the runway,

I close my eyes.

I allow time and space to run through me,

cleansing my body of his residue.

I imagine James standing at the gate,

feeling the rejection of my not looking back to wave him goodbye.

*Goodbye, James.*

*You cannot hurt us anymore.*

*Only you can make yourself well.*

To avoid another swarm of fear from rising, I shift my attention to my present and the flight attendant standing a few rows ahead of me.

I set my focus on her.

She is addressing her precious cargo with the memorized safety procedures, and like a reminder from the Universe telling me why I need never look back, she looks directly at me:

"Please secure your own mask before assisting others,"
she instructs.
She dons a yellow demo oxygen mask and pulls the tabs to secure it
tightly to her face.
*I get it!*
*This is the reason I was with him!*
*This is what I had to learn by experiencing this journey!*
I feel a rush of weightlessness lift my deflated body as the plane
begins to careen down the runway.
I smile with gratitude.
I look out of my west-facing window.
I see the sunset,
red and glowing
on the tip of the wing
and I inhale.

# Chant for the Caretaker

*Caretaker, caretaker what do you need?*
*Caretaker, caretaker just watch me bleed*
*Love maker, love maker watch me now suffer*
*Love maker, love maker feed me last supper*
*Bread breaker, bread breaker do as you please*
*Bread breaker, bread breaker 'cause I'm now on my knees*
*Peace maker, peace maker I set you free*
*Peace maker, peace maker grace be with thee.*

by Robert Buffler
an incredible poet of
Migratory Words
Canmore, Alberta

# A Song for James

# I Never Knew Your Love (Could Hurt Like This)

*Tonight I'm aching for you, Baby.*
*My heart's been breaking for you lately.*
*I can't escape this bitter night,*
*I lay here fighting for the right.*
*I need to know where you may be,*
*So I can finally make you see*
*There's more to life than living*
*It's taking with some giving!*

**Chorus 1:**
*But there's only so much I can do,*
*I just cannot understand you*
*You've been a part of me so long,*
*I don't know where we went wrong*
*And there's only so much I can say,*
*There's just got to be a way*
*I miss your voice, your touch, your kiss*
*But I never knew your love could hurt like this.*

*As your mind takes you from me, Darlin',*
*I'm feeling all hope slowly fallin'.*
*I would beg, and plead, and pray,*
*just for your hands to touch my face.*
*And though I cannot always be*
*the one that everyone else sees*
*if you would look me in the eye*
*we could drop this thin disguise.*

**Chorus 2:**
*But there's only so much I can do,*
*I just cannot do it for you*

*You've been a part of me so long,*
*Holding on to you is wrong*
*And there's only so much I can say,*
*I've just got to go my own way*
*I miss your love and tenderness*
*But I never knew your love could hurt like this.*
*Instrumental Solo….*

**Bridge:**

*So many years have passed us by*
*Too many tears I've had to cry*
*You're already gone, an empty shell*
*Well, I'm choosing Heaven, not this hell!*

**Chorus 3:**

*And there's only so much I can do,*
*I just have to walk away from you*
*You've been a part of me so long,*
*Holding on to me is wrong*
*And there's only so much I can say,*
*You've just got to find your own way*
*I miss your voice, your touch, your kiss,*
*I miss your love and tenderness*
*A sweet goodbye is all I wish*
*But I never knew your love could hurt like this*
*I never knew your love could*
*Hurt.*
*Like.*
*This.*

A Message from Colleen

Hello, I am Colleen Songs, the alter ego of the woman 'INHALE' is about.

It has taken a lot of time and blind faith to write this story.

You see, it's not an easy one to write.

With mental illness and suicide so prevalent over the years I was afraid to speak out from the point of view of the loved one or Caregiver.

How could I make clear the reality of 'living inside the life of' this cruel and lethal dis-ease of the mind?

There is so much information and support nowadays for the patient, but what is there for the Caregivers?

There may be lots of support now, (and I urge you to seek it out) but at the time this happened to me, there was none.

When I would ask about whether my Children and I should stay or leave, to seek some sort of wisdom in my state of panic and blur, I was only asked the same rhetorical question by every therapist and counsellor...

"You wouldn't leave your husband if he had cancer, would you?"

We barely understood what was really happening, but we were expected to endure this terminal suffering?

I was hushed.

I was told not to say how I really felt for fear of thrusting him deeper into a tirade, manic depression, or worse... suicide.

So I stayed silent, only telling bits and pieces to my dearest and closest confidants.

I would try to sleep at night with sorrow buried in my heart.

Every day trying to stay positive while skidding along the edge of broken glass.

I was naïve to the vast array of abuse that a narcissistic personality procures and what the fine line was between narcissism and mental illness.

Abuse to me meant physical beatings or cheating on your spouse.

I didn't real-eyes that abuse included multiple levels of psychological control and manipulation.

From intimacy to verbal comments.

Isolation to public embarrassment.

I believe that everyone should read this story.

Caregivers and families of loved ones with mental illness are not supported enough.

We're not given the honest, eye-opening truth.

Without truth one does not have the means to make the best decisions.

A quote from this book says it all:

"Thought is the smallest particle of creation. When it becomes dis-eased it becomes a warped sense of reality where the dwellers who love you reside."

After finally leaving him I spent months pouring it out on paper through songwriting, my medium of expression which I have always used to purge my thoughts.

Songs tumbled upon each other like a mass of metal in a wrecking yard.

Some songs were angry.

Some songs were heartbreaking.

Some remain hastily written phrases I can barely understand, doodled webs of scribbles, or torn and crumpled pieces of rubble screaming from the bottom of my trash can.

But no matter how many songs I wrote to release the pain, the story kept nagging at me to be told.

The songs weren't enough.

I had to get the words alone literally out of my body!

No amount of music could soften them.

I had to take the chance and tell my story in a way that would help the readers feel the feelings, imagine the hidden torment, and become more aware of those who are left unheard.

To encourage you to listen to those "little red flags," demand being heard when you ask for help as the Caregiver, especially when Children are involved.

As I began to write the words began to take shape and I became lighter and freer.

Those who know me are stunned by my story, and quite honestly, so am I!

She was another woman entirely from the one I am now, but without her I wouldn't be where I am today.

Time heals, but in the words of Maya Angelou: "There is no greater agony than a story kept hidden inside you."

It simply torments you.

So on February 19, 2013,

in our present place where we both felt safe,

we set our fear aside and reached deep within the heart of Colleen.

Together we sat down at my desk and I allowed her story to flow through the best format she knew:

Lyric and prose.

We left emotion to form the melody.

I used my talent of wordsmithing

as her source of bravery

and she opened up.

One word at a time.

I wrote from the moment,

by sharing the thoughts that kept her there

and the love that kept her going.

I prayed regularly for honesty and clarity as so many memories and periods of time were lost to her.

I wove several experiences into one.

One chapter at a time.

I cried with every paragraph

and still cry when I read it

but with fresher eyes,

a lighter heart,
and a sense of freedom from the telling of it.
And I hope it can answer that imminent question that every
abusee receives:
"Why did you stay?"
Sharing her thought patterns was the only way I could answer that
curious, judgmental enquiry.
"Just tell the story," I would encourage her every time fear
would arise.
There are memories still locked in a bowl of jello, too congealed in
that foggy pool called 'autopilot' that she had to live on for so long.
One by one they were buried, peacefully trusting that the
memories that did come to light would help someone else find
their courage.
Names and locations have been changed to free those who were
involved and to protect her from those not too happy about my
writing this story.
That's why it took me so long to begin:
worried about what others might think.
You can't make everyone happy.
You can only be the best you that YOU can be
and stand on your truth.
This story is meant to open Your eyes to the outside circle
around You,
to the Ones looking in,
lifting You,
feeding You,
keeping vigilance over You;
the ones affected by Your every breath,
and the ones on the invisible sidelines of each and every one of Us.
I hope to make them visible.

I hope to provide comfort and encouragement

that You are not alone,
that You are understood,
that You cannot do the work for another human being.

I write to remind You to breathe...
to "secure your own mask before assisting others."
For You I share this story...
In sickness and in health.

*With Love, Colleen*

Colleen Songs is a Canadian-born-and-raised 'Writer of Word and Song'. From writing her first song at the age of 14 to aide her communication with elderly parents, to currently working on her career as a professional musician and hired ' Wordsmith', Colleen has written her way through adolescence, love, heartbreak, back to love, motherhood, trauma, loss, self-discovery and joy.

Inspiring listeners through song and empowering readers through word, Colleen aims to sing the song of the Caregiver, the unsung melody, to free them of guilt, fear and loss of hope. Her motto of "Dreams Never Expire" follows her wherever she goes to encourage lost souls to use their unique gifts and talents to love themselves back to life.

You can follow her at www.colleensongs.com

Photo credits: Cover: Colleen's photo taken with her little point-and-shoot camera on her actual flight from Yuma. Outside Back Cover Author Photo: Clay Neddo of Clay Neddo Photography. Bio/Author Page Photo: Peter Gold of Gold Photography.

CPSIA information can be obtained
at www.ICGtesting.com
Printed in the USA
LVHW01s0136100118
562491LV00001B/10/P